MW00561220

Tao

of

Surfing

Finding Depth
at Low Tide

– Michael A. Allen –

Library of Congress Cataloging-in-Publication Data

Allen, Michael A., 1963—
    Tao of Surfing : finding depth at low tide / Michael A. Allen.
        p.   cm.
    ISBN 1-56825-057-6
    1. Tao. 2. Life. 3. Philosophy, Taoist. I. Title.
B127.T3A55 1996
181'.114--dc20   96-15408
                                                                        CIP

Tao of Surfing:
Finding Depth at Low Tide
by Michael A. Allen

Copyright © 1997 by Michael Allen
Second Printing, 2000

Cover Photograph by Michael A. Allen. Cover and interior design by
Betsy A. Lampé. Photographs courtesy of the author, Michael A. Allen.
All photos are copyrighted and may not be reprinted without the ex-
press, written permission of the author. Author Photo courtesy of Julie
M. Allen.

Published by Rainbow Books, Inc.
P. O. Box 430
Highland City, FL 33846-0430 USA
Editorial Offices Telephone: (863) 648-4420
Direct-Order Telephone (800) 431-1579

In Memory of and in Dedication to Richard Hynes –
A Great & Powerful Surfer,
Who Rides along My Side
With the Majestic Grace of the Dolphin,
Who Taught Me that I need Search No More.

Acknowledgments

To Wayne Okamoto and Steve Irvin for providing wave riding vehicles over the years, allowing me to dance gracefully over the reef. To Jerry Johnston, tribal elder, for being there through high and low tide. And to the groomsmen, Kevin Fujimoto, John Hohn and David Moses. To those who surfed faithfully by my side through the icy winters and balmy summers. To all those who gave their unbiased opinion to me after reviewing various stages of the manuscript. And in memory of Gary Babcock, whose numerous editorial comments proved invaluable toward polishing the final draft. To Betty Wright who believed in my dream. To my lovely wife Julie for her continued support and belief in me, and in us. To those who have appeared before me when I needed them most. And to those who continue the journey, exploring the deeper meanings of our existence.

Contents

Foreword

The title of this book has been here from the beginning. It came from the depth of who Michael is as a human being and is nurtured by his academic studies and writing on the subject of comparative East-West philosophy and his travel in China. The title was set — the book, and its purpose, remained far in the future.

Over the last ten years, Michael made three previous attempts at writing this book. Each was finally abandoned. There was a feeling that something else was waiting to be grasped. Then, without prior expectation, Michael was suddenly immersed in an intense personal experience, with a promise made and kept, that provided a purpose and a reason for this book. As a result, Michael, in my humble opinion, experienced great personal growth and also found his voice as a writer.

What could be more Western than a California surfer? What could be more Eastern than Taoist wisdom? Can East and West, shaped by unique personal experience, ever meet? Perhaps, like those most ultimate of perceived opposites, life and death, they were never truly separate . . . Please pause and consider that last sentence again — more slowly.

Dichotomy may be a grand illusion, no more than a temporary failing of our human comprehension. Finding depth at low tide means reaching a greater understanding of the events that shape our lives, even the events that happen at low tide, when the flow may not be in accord with our desires. Getting through the roughest of times with enhanced knowledge of the Self and the world in which we live allows us to recognize that the simplest actions can be the most profound, most revealing and most growth producing.

A father looks forward to teaching his son. As Michael Allen's father, let me here express my profound gratitude for all that my son, with true Eastern filial piety, has taught me.

– Donn A. Allen

Introduction

Tao of Surfing begins the journey into Self with rich naturalistic metaphor and vivid imagery along the coastal roads and beaches between Big Sur and San Francisco, examining how nature is always in a state of continuous change. The metaphor notes the changes between the land and sea and the changes that we ourselves undergo through-out our lives. Death, then, is not an end but another phase in the process of transformation, ultimately a new beginning.

Fulfilling a promise to my brother, I paddled his longboard into the Pacific Ocean and dispersed his ashes into the waves. As I scattered the ashes into the calm wa-ters of the bay, the mystery of Tao began to unravel. The essence of this journey is to understand the meaning behind the waves of life, the metaphorical vicissitudes that create the journey itself.

Dancing upon the wave, light, free, barely touching the surface, the maneuvers become more fluid, more powerful, and yet less energy is exerted while continuously heighten-ing one's sensibilities. The essence of Tao is Wu-Wei, ef-fortless action, a flowing movement whose motion continues forward to a new plateau. We also come to understand the importance of our interaction with the environment, which is essential for our continued existence in both a literal and a symbolic sense. The roads I travel and the waves I search for and ride exemplify the flowing movement and continuous change of life itself.

Chapter One also exposes nakedness, displaying it as a metaphor that captures the essence of revealing oneself to the world. By the same account, the metaphor is also symbolic of shedding external phenomena, dispelling beliefs that hinder our continued progression. Interaction becomes something that not only exists with the interplay of our surroundings but becomes apparent within the Self, our "Interactive Self." Throughout the chapter, an in depth search into the meaning of Tao continues along with the search for the meaning of our "interactive" existence. The emphasis also remains on simplicity, reaching into the well of minimalist philosophy as did some architectural designers in the 19th century. This model of simplicity can only be compared with the Platonic Ideal in that it is always something worth striving for as an "Ideal State." Unlike Plato's philosophy, however, Taoist simplicity is obtainable and depends solely on one's own free-willed actions.

Chapter Two takes place with my brother Rick in his final hours with AIDS. It was written while I was beside him, up all hours of the night, writing in an attempt to capture the immediate, spontaneous moment with uninterrupted flow. As with the entire book, there is a certain style that transforms the past to the immediate present as if this were all happening as we speak. These are the actual pages taken from the original journal entries written under the simmering desert heat of New Mexico. Within this chapter I expose the post traumatic stress that resulted from the ordeal. My mind runs rampant and I am no longer able to think clearly throughout the night. Finally after numerous nights of interrupted sleep, a dream pervades my sleeping consciousness. Within the dream I myself face death in an attempt to uncover the very thing causing the destruction of my inner peace. It was as if I took the fear from my brother so that he could go on his journey peacefully. In the aftermath of the dream, I awake to find that I ultimately defeated death itself and that my peacefulness and "Natural State" was again restored.

Chapter Three utilizes the wave metaphor to its fullest. The philosophical investigation searches for answers illuminating our interaction with nature, and with our surroundings. A vivid example displays the waves passing over the reef affecting each other, shaping each other and ultimately defining each other's existence. The search to define an ocean wave's entity begins to define our own autonomous existence, indicative of freedom towards continued "on the road" self-cultivation so that "The distance and places I travel are purely dependent upon my will." This chapter also takes us to the ceremony where Rick's ashes were taken into the waves. Amidst the ceremony, instilled reflection takes us on a journey to examine the meaning behind Rick's ashes as they floated in a plume of dust under the water. This ultimately leads to continued exploration into defining our own existence, questioning what entities create our unique individuality.

Chapter Four summarizes and synthesizes the gathered information, making sense of all the data. Finally, a conclusion is drawn. Like the waves and the reef, there was also an interaction on the same level between my brother and the waves he rode. They too shaped each other and ultimately defined each other's very existence. With that, a new definition of Taoism emerges. "Tao is pure interaction, not harmony of opposing forces, but interactive qualities that support each other, and nurture each other in a symbiotic sense." Finally, the realization crystallizes that my brother never really left. He has returned to his original state, the pure interactive state of Being, to the waves themselves. Like us, my brother's journey has not ended. It has merely begun.

Chapter One

Rubái

The Cresting Wave Addresses Now the Land,
With Beauty, Grace and Power Beyond Command.
In Courage Seize Thy Moment in its Grasp.
Mourn Not a Glory that Expires in Sand.

– D. A. Allen

I remember surfing until the ball of orange flames dipped down into the water's edge. It was a minus tide, with the wind, warm, still offshore, and the waves, some of the best I've ever seen. The sun sank slowly in the distance as an enormous moon emerged from behind the cliffs. Bright. Clear. Surfing on moonlit water, dancing over the reef, risking injury, and challenging our instincts to reach heights never before attained. Pushing us to the extremes and finding depth at low tide.

There it was before me, the harsh reality that we were not going to be surfing together forever. Being out there in the lineup, looking over at each other, offshore wind in our hair, sets rolling in from the ocean depths, it seemed that we'd never get older. As children, we felt immortal, invincible, and as we grew, we gained an uncanny ability to understand the ocean swells, the weather patterns, and the effects the moon had on the tides. No worries. A time of reflection on the beaches that made us who we were. The waves and changing tides not only shaped the sand but shaped our lives along with it. The passing of each day always presented something new. The understanding of our environment became essential, not only for predicting waves, but for self-preservation as well.

There are times when I think we'll surf forever, that moments exist where time stands still, and the ageless beauty of youthful souls will forever relax in the warmth of the midday sun. I alone have been caught up in my corporeal invincibility, escaping the mere idea of man's temporal nature. Not until we experience death do we realize that we are mortal beings who must one day face this reality, like the Samurai Warriors who understood this well and then went on — without fear.

As the tides flow back and forth, the seasons change, and the swells continue rolling into the bay. The elements of death and rebirth here are a continuum.

When we were young, never was there a day where the sun didn't touch the nakedness of our skin. We lived outdoors in the vastness of nature. Never did we think that we'd get older, that we'd move away, that some of us would quit surfing, or that some of us would die early on.

The winds that blow so freely across the ocean arrive upon the shores of the bay. Now the wind is barely noticeable and the sun overlooking the California coast has drenched the sand with warmth and brilliance. Light reflects off of the textured sand, bringing me peacefully into a dreamy state of relaxed intoxication. J realize that J'm never separated from my environment, and that somehow J'm a part of this pure interaction. My hair lightens and my skin darkens with each passing moment. The state of continuous change is inescapable. J see it in the waves. J see it in myself.

J lift my head from my pillow of sand. Another wave rolls gently to shore, eventually disappearing between the infinite grains on this desolate beach.

As a small child, most waves towered over me. Paddling out on a big day at a familiar place was instrumental toward igniting a fear that took years to overcome. Outside sets stormed toward the beach, pushing their way along the rock jetty. The first one broke in front of me, pushing me down to the bottom, holding me there with a giant hand controlling my destiny. Struggling free from imposed barriers J slipped out of the turbulence and up to the surface gasping for air. Out of breath, J looked to the outside and saw that there were more to come. Again and again J was pushed to the bottom. Fortunately, J was also pushed toward shore, finally reaching the surface. Able to retrieve my board, J turned toward the beach and used the waves' energy to take me in, finding safety in the shallower waters along the shoreline. A great fear of big waves engulfed me that day. J felt that J had come closer to death than ever before. A cool breeze, drifting offshore ran through me in spite of my wet suit, chilling me deep within. J left the beach that day feeling defeated, scared and cold. Jt wasn't until years later that J again faced death — and ultimately defeated my fear of it. And it was then that my natural state was again restored.

Taoism teaches that death is as natural as the four seasons. Life and death are one, and their succession, like day and night, follows the natural course of things. So then, why was J so fearful and of what was J so afraid? This is the question J now contemplated.

Reflection begins at the death of my brother, a fellow wave rider. Reflections are instilled into my mind and into the small pools that form over the reef at low tide. Trauma alone should not be responsible for instilling such reflection. Unreflective pools like an unreflective life, have no depth. An unreflective life diminishes possibilities for personal exploration. Although many live "happily" in this unreflective state, they do so in the shallowness of eternal safety. Eventually, it is the painful events that stir some of us to become self-reflective. We must look at pain in its positive light as a selection of reality that can aid our self-cultivation.

The waves seem to be picking up again. J grab my board and paddle out. The water seems cooler than it was earlier, but the sun has been out for a while, and J know that only my skin temperature has changed.

J remember early mornings in the middle of winter, seeing the frost-covered wood railing along the cliff, making our way onto the beach, and jumping into that cold water with only hints of light scattered across the bay.

My body once again adjusts to the new environment. Being back in the water feels good and no longer feels so cold. The initial shock has long worn off. As I look to the outside I see a set of waves rolling in around the point. Amidst my excitement, I easily forget the temperature change I'm experiencing. I squint my eyes to keep out the glare as I search for waves. The midday sun is extremely bright, reflecting off the surrounding water. Somehow I've managed to keep my hair dry. But now I'd like to get on a wave that promises at some point to plunge me unexpectedly into the cool water. Being faced with the unexpected adds to my understanding of this ever changing reality.

Now, after so many years of surfing, it is very rare that I fall off my board. Either I have reached a stage where perfect balance has become an innate quality, or I've simply reached a point where I've mastered the moves that were once new to me. I think it's the latter, realizing that it's time now to progress farther and prepare myself for a few spills to come.

Standing on the beach again, I absorb the direction of the swells. This will give me a better indication of what points are breaking. I check the tide; it's rising fast. Although some areas along the point will begin to break, there are places along the cliff-line that can pose great difficulties when one is trying to exit the water, especially with the tide rising as fast as it is. Obviously, to surf we must get wet, but both a little hindsight and a little foresight now may save us from some possibly dangerous situations later. The interaction with nature does not have to be a mindless venture, where we plunge unknowingly into the dark abyss of ignorance. Knowing the ways of nature adds to the experience, resulting in far greater immersion. The greatest depth comes about through the totality of an informed experience.

Over the centuries we have separated ourselves from what we observe, thinking that the objects in view are somehow totally separate and distinct from us. In so doing, we have separated ourselves from nature. We've made the distinction between life and death and pulled ourselves away from the very thing that sustains us. Total immersion cannot come about through separation. Involvement entails removing the distinction that separates us in the first place.

It has begun to rain. I noticed the clouds approaching this morning and felt the wind changing direction. The air gradually became cooler, and the glassy ocean plane dissipated, transforming into a granulated surface. I knew these changes were indicators of large waves to come, perhaps sometime in the night. That's how it seemed, how it always seemed, even as a child. The swells would march in during the night more often than not. At an earlier age I wondered if the waves could ever suddenly pick up during the day from a new swell. And, of course, I found out that they could. One morning the waves nearly doubled in size in only an hour. It was then I realized that the swells waited for no one. They came in when they pleased, leaving the mystery of darkness behind.

The rain continues into another day, but lessens in severity. The sun rises above the bay and the clouds begin to clear. The air is still. Mist rises from the soaked ground resting below the towering redwoods. The forest overlooks the bay and if the trees could see, they would be the first to spot the incoming swells. The view is beautiful at this height.

As I walk among these giants, I feel a sense of nature's grandeur. I slip deeper into the forest and reemerge in the background like a Taoist in a Chinese landscape painting. Here the sense of where I am in nature becomes self-evident. We can never take control of nature. Those who make that vain attempt constantly struggle, and continuously battle, usually with detrimental results. Nature voices its response to the invasion by creating havoc. But Taoism embraces the flow. Strength lies in working with nature rather than attempting to overcome it.

Riding a wave exemplifies this flow, the natural course of things. Here the natural course is the wave direction as it follows the contour of the ocean bottom. The wave is in a constant state of change, bending, breaking, pushing forward, duplicating the contoured bottom that it's riding above. The mirrored images in the wave do not seek to overcome. They roll along until being greeted by shore.

In all things, there is a harmony in opposites. With any extreme there will be an opposite extreme to counteract or balance it. The seemingly perfect days in surfing seem to come only when we willingly seek adverse conditions, when we paddle out when no one else would even consider it. There are those who wait for the perfect day, and they wait and wait, and, for them, it never comes. The waves arrive, and those who procrastinate will never be there to meet the incoming swells. Taoism teaches us that interaction is the key. How we interact with our surroundings determines the Way. However, our initial interaction is with ourselves. It is from ourselves that all else flows.

Suddenly we begin finding ourselves, a search within — instigated by a brief moment of reflection over a glassy surface, becoming intoxicated from the salt water wine. Nature's brew, drunk with elation. Introspection sparks a new discovery. The Self. What do we do with it? Where do we go? Develop the Self and one develops relations with the world. Taoist wandering through eternal optimism; though never straying from reality — understanding the element of uncertainty. Is anything really certain? Should it even matter? Searching for waves is part of the personal exploration as we searched deeper into our souls to reveal the inner truth that once lay hidden. Self-revealing, tide pools of the mind absorb energy, holding the once hidden knowledge, releasing it at will.

The search for waves brought forth a strength, a strength necessary to reveal a truth about who we were and what we were becoming. The reality of it all stood before us, that what we were becoming, the shaping of our lives lay latent in all our actions. These were the things we chose to do. These were the life experiences that became symbolic for generations to come. What we had to realize was that in choosing our actions, we created ourselves. Who we became was up to us.

When we're young, life is a flux of spontaneous moments. Our actions, our thoughts, our ideas take place naturally, in the sense that whatever comes about does so without any effort. Unfortunately, as many of us grow older, we tend to lose our youthful spontaneity, but only if we let it happen. J remember some of the best days' surfing, taking off on a moments' notice to check out places that might have waves. There was always a thrill to the adventure, to the sudden action taken, to decisions being made that would change the course of history, our history. We were the ones who created history for ourselves. History was in the making in each and every moment that we created it. On some of these days that seemed so perfect, J don't know if the waves themselves were actually more spectacular, or if it was driving to an unknown destination, arriving at an unfamiliar place, and surfing a new break, that added the magic to the atmosphere. Fortunately, we did take photographs on a few of these ventures, and yes, the waves were as good as J remember, but so was the magic that only spontaneity could bring.

Perspectives may change as we grow. A once large wave rolling up onto the shore is no longer intimidating, and a quality wave is just that, both ageless and eternal and will be, forever, a quality wave.

Nakedness exposes, it reveals — that which is so often covered up. Truth lies below the surface, beneath the rhetoric. Waves are formed by the contour of the land that lies below the surface, rarely seen, rarely touched. Without inhibition, innocence is revealed. Paddling toward the sun as it began to appear from behind the forest covered hills, J looked back toward the beach only to see a woman slowly entering the cool and seemingly motionless early morning waters of the bay. The tide low, the reef was exposed as was she in all her beautiful nakedness. In an instant, like a sudden flash of insight, I perceived the beauty in being naked. Therein lay spontaneity and fearlessness that revealed underlying truth. The power of the moment lay bound in the fearlessness to present what is most often hidden, an ability to go beyond the rigidity of structured norms that only bind us farther from deeper meaning. This total exposure also allows us to return to the natural state. No barriers, no walls to inhibit the pure interaction with nature itself. Nakedness stands as a metaphor and symbol of the raw material that gave rise to our sensitive nature. I realized too that it was this sensitivity from being vulnerable that brought forth the pure understanding and awareness necessary to go beyond societal walls.

As small children we are able to express nakedness in its purest form. There is something to be said about being naked outdoors, feeling the sun, the wind, and the ocean without any obstruction. There is a certain freedom and excitement to exposing oneself to natural surroundings. Emerging from the ocean's shore, the water gently rolls off the skin, cleansing the soul, renewing and revitalizing the spirit within. If Taoism emphasizes the return to the natural state, then perhaps nakedness symbolizes the removing of exterior phenomena that inhibit this process.

In the afternoon I stood on the beach and felt the warm offshore wind. It seemed to pass through me, gently warming the surface of my skin, then touching the essence of my soul, and continuing out across the ocean surface into the bay. The waters that day appeared aquamarine like the tropical waters of the Caribbean. The sky held intense

shades of blue and the clouds wandered like balls of cotton that had pulled free from their stems. Bits of salt and grains of sand slowly gathered onto my oil-drenched skin. Each breath was slow and deep, and my mind was free to reflect at will. In the distance appeared a sailboat moving across the horizon at a slow but observable pace. Another wave pushed itself up the steep embankment only to return to that from which it came.

Over the years, I finally understood why it was that I could not stay away from the waves. Somehow, being back in the waves always brings me a sense of revitalization. The environment here along the central coast is raw, and most of it is still in its natural state. In the middle of winter, I feel some of my greatest peace, riding alone, even when the wind chill brings the air temperature into the thirties. Mist hangs heavily along the tree line after settling there during the night. It seems as though I'm surfing in the mountains at some place high above sea level. But this is where the forest meets the beach. And this is where I've come to ride.

The most unpredictable weather heightens my state of awareness. Unpredictability alone provides the avenues to realize our place in nature. When we welcome the unexpected, we have begun the dance of the flowing movement.

One morning, while riding along the point, the sky opened up, and through the freezing air fell balls of hail the size of marbles. A hundred yards from shore, I turned my board around, dropped in, shot down the line, and protected

my face from the pellets of ice. I paddled in and sought
shelter on the beach, under the wooden stairway until the
storm had passed. In minutes the storm ended, revealing
the sun with all its warmth and beauty. I enjoyed the sudden extreme changes in weather. I knew from looking north
that no one else was out, but loneliness never entered my
consciousness. Although the chill was in the air, the sun's
warming rays penetrated my wetsuit. The air seemed still
and motionless. I could hear nothing, as if I was removed
from it all, yet here I felt closer to nature than ever; even as
the waves rolled in and the wind blew offshore, I sensed a
deep and perfect stillness. This was stillness in motion, perfect harmony amidst continuous change.

Perhaps this exemplified Wu-Wei, riding a powerful
wave while harnessing the wave's energy, wasting nothing,
conserving everything. One morning it came to me. I
dropped into an outside wave rolling through the point. I
had to race the section through the shallow spots and in
doing so, I found that my body barely moved, but within me
there was a rhythm as if I were dancing upon the wave.
I've never experienced anything quite like this in all my years
of surfing. I continued down the line, pushing farther and
farther, building up speed, racing it all the way. I rode until
there was no wave left. I tapped into the movement of the
wave and followed it with precision. My body felt nearly still.
Dancing the flowing movement had been effortless, and yet
there was the most power and speed. There is nothing like it.

It's mid-June, and still the rain storms come. Only a couple weeks back, there was still more snowfall in the Sierras. But the storms don't last long now, and soon after, the sun appears. It's warmer than ever. Tourists can be seen on the beaches. Now some of the days are too hot for me. Heat attracts crowds to beaches that were once deserted. I study the people who only see these beaches in summer and wonder if they have any idea what the winters are like. A river must be crossed to get farther up the beach. Now, however, this particular river is dry and people walk across it almost without notice. Even in the fall they still cross with ease. Some of the trees that once lined the top of the cliff are gone as well. Last winter's rain eroded the topsoil enough to allow them to break free and fall to the beach below, where they were eventually swept away by the waves. Winter brings about the most change. But somehow there are also times of perfect stillness – quietude and peacefulness. In winter, the sun is gentler, the wind more crisp, and the ocean more mysterious.

The waves during winter have a taste all their own. Their look and feel are unique. But those who see these beaches only in summer never know this. Never do they experience the beauty and gracefulness, the raw power of rolling energy originating miles from shore. I see an emptiness in these people, an emptiness stemming from an unfamiliarity with their surroundings. Perhaps their emptiness is from the lack of knowledge that exists in so many of us. I certainly can't blame them for not understanding all this. They're not here to experience it. I've chosen to live here, for now, and experience as much as I can. If they had a

desire to understand, a desire to become familiar with nature's constant movement and change, then there would be no emptiness. <u>Emptiness seems to be in the faces of those who lack curiosity, who live their routine lives in an unknowing, unreflective way.</u> How can anyone live in an unreflective state, lacking the flowing movement where knowledge becomes stagnant and unpliable?

The knowledge I speak of can only be obtained by increasing one's awareness and immersing ourselves in the environment. In no other way is this knowledge obtainable. To understand the ocean, we must be close to it, close enough to feel the water, to smell the ocean breeze, to taste the salt that settles onto one's skin. Our senses become involved, our mind is alert and aware of constant change.

I'm up before the sun rises. Dawn has always been a special time of the day for me. The air is usually calmer, the gentle breeze is offshore, and the moon illuminates, slowly making its way down below the horizon. This morning I walked to the water's edge. For some reason the air was calmer than normal, the ocean quieter, and a fog bank sat ominously offshore as if waiting to strike at the right moment. Out of the fog appeared an old ship that sat quietly and seemed lifeless. Although the ship appeared abandoned, I sensed someone was aboard. I headed up the point along the beach, looking back occasionally to see if the ship would disappear back into the fog.

The fog began to clear as the sun broke through. The rising sun represents a renewal, where life begins a new day.

Paddling out in the dark is best, especially on the clear mornings where, in the distance, the faintest trails of sunlight can be seen bending over the horizon. The colors are more brilliant before the crimson glow actually appears. Even the slightest amount of dust in the air filters those first rays into incredibly rich shades of orange, red and yellow.

As a child, getting up to surf before the sun rose was the way I chose to begin a new day. Perhaps I felt I was ahead of things if I was up before the sun, because I knew that if the sun got up before I did, I would feel that I had missed something great. The sun became a symbol to me as to the Shinto who worship it as a symbol of life. Early morning was always quiet and still to the point of being motionless. I remember feeling this same stillness late at night as well, but inside I knew differently. In the morning, upon awakening, I knew the cool ocean water would be refreshing and exhilarating. While in the late night hours nothing could exhilarate me except the dreams that would flow with me throughout the night.

I worked my way to the tip of the point and paddled out. The ship sat there, motionless. The waves were small but well shaped. One can't expect too much size, for it is summer now and the swells don't carry with them the power that accompanies winter. Power is seasonal. Different swells stem from changing weather patterns. As for the surfers, we simply ride along, following the continuous change in weather throughout the year, following a natural course like a stream winding its way down the mountain for the first time when the snow begins to thaw.

When cool water meets warm air, fog appears along the coast. Sometimes I hear the fog horn in the middle of the night. These are the nights that begin warm and balmy. If the waves have been small for a week or so, the lack of activity gives the water a chance to warm up. The fog horn announces that a new swell has hit, disturbing the once motionless surface, cooling the water temperature. J already know the following morning will be cooler than the previous day, both in the water and out. On some days past, fog brought forth a feeling of something cold, lonely and forbidding. But that was a time of long ago, when for a brief period J was detached from the land itself.

On one excursion J traveled south and stopped at a break known to be localized. J had a difficult time with this term let alone the events that took place actualizing the term itself. J thought, how could anyone surf and do so peacefully when they feel they have some need to protect something that isn't theirs to begin with? Protective of what? J asked myself. They weren't like the environmentalists who protect the land for the sake of itself and for future generations to come. They weren't really protecting anything, but were rather attempting to take over a spot that would remain long after they were dead, gone, and forgotten. All that would remain of them is a bad memory of a destructive attitude that has no positive effect on the land or its people. They, most of all, were the most disconnected from the land they thought they were so close to. J thought it peculiar how these individuals could be acting with such great disregard for their environment and their fellow man in often very destructive ways.

The state of ignorance is the farthest from Tao. It creates greater disharmony, like the attitude carried with localism. To follow the Tao, there must be the understanding. Ignorance destroys, it creates disharmony from the mere futile ambitions of the weak minded. Strength through knowledge, knowledge of the Way, restores the natural state.

Unlike Taoists, they never understood the great interaction with the environment. If you think for an instant that the things around us don't affect us, then you're sadly mistaken. I knew that these people must have been adversely affected somewhere else, from neglectful parents, from lack of supervision at a young age, from being a child given everything except the things that really matter like time, love, patience and understanding. There was hostility within these people that drove them farther from the land.

There are so many who have everything and yet have nothing spiritual, meaningful and lasting. My minimalist ways have allowed me to freely express Taoist principles. The result is freedom, mobility and spontaneity. Having less in the way of material things opens up another world, a world that is not so fixed and rigid. Seeing all these materially wealthy kids who have been given it all made me understand their attitude in and out of the water. Having been spoon fed everything since day one, they lack a basic and necessary appreciation. There was emptiness where a value system should have existed. So there they sat, some now in their mid-thirties, yelling obscenities at those on the beach or on the cliff line to go home, to stay away, to go anywhere else except there. It was a gang mentality of protecting their turf for unsound reasons. We've been lead to believe that gangs

✢

generally originate in a poor environment, where kids learn to grab whatever they can as a means to survival. Here was this same style expressed by the "Well-to-do". At first, I couldn't comprehend what I was witnessing. It all seemed so irrational. We sometimes witness behavior so removed from what we would consider rational that we don't see what is actually going on. I witnessed someone old enough to know better throwing rocks over the cliff at surfers making their way down the trail. I watched in disbelief. This was so far from the ways of Taoism that it shook me for a moment. I sadly realized that this was a reality I had to deal with.

What perhaps shook me even more was that the surfers themselves were victims of this same mentality. Where usually I feel peacefulness in the water, here I felt none. Destructive attitudes hung motionless in the still air. There seemed nothing natural left to this landscape. Not even a sunrise here could restore this bay's lifelessness. Nature itself seemed to disappear with the devastating attitudes toward the land and the people. No longer did I see the once flourishing water birds. Nor were there any sign of the seals or dolphin that once were. Nature seemed profoundly affected by this attitude. Signs all over indicated this. Human ways and the ever so fragile ways of nature are somehow intertwined. Never can they be separated. This became apparent. Nature's delicate balances and tensions were warped by the disturbing influence of this defined interference.

The environment reflects the ways of man, good or bad, and the degree of truth to this must be realized if we are going to be able to continue in a nurturing way. Ultimately, we need to realize that we have the capacity for shaping our environment, and within each environment, inescapable interactions exist. For each of us, one particular environment is more conducive to the Way (Tao). Although for a moment we may think we are removed from our surroundings — we're not. As I travel through the inner cities, the megalopolis, I see and feel the effects of total disassociation. By contrast, as I drive closer to the smaller beach cities that line the coast, there is always a warmer feeling. Seeing the water again defuses any frustration that has built up in me while being away from the coast. Frustration dissipates into peacefulness. Tapping into the Way brings forth a greater understanding of the Self. The transformation into a life of greater peace begins as we learn the interplay existing between ourselves and our environment. I thought it possible for inner city dwellers to also feel greater peacefulness, but for this to happen they must feel close to the land they stand upon. Chaos brewed from disassociation.

The flowing movement felt when riding waves is simply a metaphor for flowing through life. When we find the environment that brings about greater peacefulness, we can perform at a higher level and deal with everyday events more calmly. When the mind is calm and totally undisturbed, we can tap into our greatest powers of reason. With a calm mind, the spirit within is revitalized, a new consciousness is realized and the deep breaths of reason continue toward a unifying principle. Nature has never left us. We have left it, and now we must return.

This morning I wake to a mixture of blue sky and dark clouds. I am not sure if rain is in the forecast. I wouldn't mind if it is. Rain would again cleanse things as well as increase the chances of a new swell.

The sun has broken through and the air temperature slowly rises along with the tide. Earlier this morning we again danced our way over a shallow reef along the point. The tide was low but not as low as we've seen it. There is an ease in walking out along the beach at low tide. The beach is exposed, allowing one to forget the days of winter. I remember when the tide was so high that getting in and back out of the water posed difficulties. At that time of the year, not only the tide but the current running along the point can be life threatening. Sometimes the waves form with precision, with the current creating long lines that speed toward shore. When this happens, we can ride some of the fastest waves ever and lock in to its flowing movement. When paddling out on some of the bigger days, I'd find a channel or a rip current allowing me to get out without exerting much energy.

Fighting against the natural course of the current is definitely a mistake. We'd even ride it out to the next point if need be and conserve our energy for where we'd really need it. Only my knowledge derived from experience gives me the confidence to proceed through the rip. Understanding the ways of nature increases my ability to ride these swells with confidence.

There is something good about being on the road. Not just traveling but actually driving the road, experiencing the land, feeling the earth beneath you. The last time I flew, I looked down. I felt profoundly separated from the land. At 30,000 feet, I couldn't clearly make out any bit of topography. I couldn't wait to get back into my truck to travel along the coast again. There is nothing like driving California's coastal highway whether or not you are searching for waves. When I head down Highway 1, I feel the ocean air against my face as I tilt my head out the window for a moment like a dog. The small bit of untouched land along side the road doesn't separate me from the waves, but rather draws me closer to them. The land, the highway, and the ocean all flow into each other seamlessly. If any barriers were to exist here, they would exist purely in one's mind and nowhere else. Here, space expands without limit. There are still areas of road along this highway where I look out across the land, and see nothing but land itself. No visible areas of modernization taint its purity. Sometimes it may be a cultivated piece of farm land where the crops are lined in rows stretching to infinity. I can see no end. Even here, farms stretch out along the ocean, along the cliff line, overlooking the great Pacific. When the sun rises here, one feels warmth penetrating the rich soil and all those who cultivate it. Sometimes it feels as if I'm traveling through a well-written novel. But this is all real, and I'm the one who has taken to the road once again to experience all that it has to offer.

I end up at a place somewhere between Morro Bay and Big Sur. The morning is cool, extremely clear and bright. This spot is a beach break, but for some reason the swell is

coming in from a sharp angle producing waves typical of point breaks. The waves are clear, thin, and so well formed that I have to take a second look.

The importance of spontaneity is becoming clearer to me. None of this was planned. We just pulled in while traveling along the coast. Some of the best days happen with minimal planning. One's mind has to be free to allow for taking off on a moment's notice and discovering without expectations. Spontaneity is the key to discovering our environment and ourselves. It invites introspection that reveals inner qualities. When one can let go of expectations and desires for things to go a certain way, then no way is the perfect way. When no way is the perfect way, how can one ever be disappointed?

Riding the road, being there, feeling each and every imperfection on this highway. I follow the dashed lines as they bend and curve. I swallow up the road as it passes beneath my truck. No looking back. I'm moving forward continuously. At a steady rate I work my way along the coast, making sure to recognize the land around me. I spot an area where I can pull over. From here the road seems endless. I guess it is if you wanted to continue on. I have a destination in mind and yet take time to see the land I travel through. Many are so focused on a destination they fail to see and appreciate what lies in between. They drive to their destination and see nothing on the way. Imagine all they are missing. Even when they arrive, they fail to appreciate where they are, being too caught up in wanting to be somewhere else again.

Every time I travel, I'm aware of these people. I move aside and let them pass. I know it's more important to let them hurry by unimpeded than to get in their way. For them, I'm merely another obstacle to be overcome. These are the same people who won't let me in when trying to change lanes. They see the blinker and speed up. These people perceive me as trying to get ahead of them, like I've taken another step past them up the corporate ladder. For them, life is struggle enough without there being more people in the way to obstruct their forward mobility. But this direction is misperceived. I see retrograde motion within this constant struggle. There is one motion and it's all backward, pushing themselves farther back in time and with it, farther into chaos.

Those drivers who do actually let you in have found an ensuing strength. They have found a strength within them-selves, a peacefulness and grace allowing them to give way. The driver I give way to is thankful. I feel good about it and we each have a better day because of it. One small move with a force to promote goodness. Somewhere there is a route, a way that eliminates entanglement. When we discover this, we can dance through obstacles like the waves that follow the contour of the reef.

Today we rode another spot for the first time. This place is nearby but for some reason no one ever seems to ride it. Perhaps it's due to this particular spot lacking accessibility. A few hundred yards of paddling up the point is the quick-est way there. On this particular morning, the fog rested

quietly just above the surface, making the cliff line barely visible from the outside. The water was warm, the air cool, and
the waves unpredictable. A peak is breaking a few hundred
yards beyond the waves rolling through the inside. Boats pass
closer than we are to the main peak. A small, lone shack sits
on the edge of the cliff, visible only from out here. The waves
are good size, producing straight-up peaks. It must be hitting
a small strip of submerged reef. If I'm off to one side by only
a few feet from the peak, I won't be able to catch the wave. At
first I think I'm out far enough until another set breaks in front
of me by at least another fifty yards. Once in a while a lone
character appears with a long, stringy beard. He never says
anything, he just rides, while that beard of his blows without a
care in the pursuing wind. He seems to have traveled from
another time and has unexpectedly been dropped into his own
future. To me he has appeared without notice and disappears
without a trace, leaving the same way he came.

Through trial and error I make my way out to where I
should be if I am going to catch any of these set waves. My
companion follows my lead and meets me out here. He finds
out, too, the importance of timing and positioning. One has
to be lined up in the right spot to catch the wave. To be in
the right spot depends not only on the flowing movement, but
upon knowledge of waves and the ability to tune into new
surroundings. There is a synthesis of knowledge and intu-
ition that is being put to use here.

There are always indescribable feelings whenever I
paddle into an unfamiliar spot. I certainly have greater confidence when I approach new situations than when I was
younger, but the excitement of the unknown will always be

with me even as it was when I was a child. Only now it's better, because as I grow older, my ability to respond to the unknown becomes increasingly more flexible. The real test of our flexibility comes when we are faced with something entirely new. I do not believe that rigidity must occur naturally with increasing age. On the contrary, I think the mind can become as resilient as we want if we continue the mental exercises necessary for this upkeep.

Taoist philosophy exemplifies flowing movement and promotes a type of exercise that allows for the continued maintenance of the mind, the very source of this movement. Buddhists believe that one must empty the mind. Taoist philosophy, however, emphasizes the strengthening of the mind by emptying unnecessary thoughts that blind us to the Way.

Unnecessary thought is like unnecessary movement; it wastes energy and often complicates and detracts from natural movement. Watch a group of surfers and you'll see one out of the crowd who gets into waves easier, flows down the line faster, makes nearly impossible sections, and does all this effortlessly. Directing this movement is power and gracefulness that is never fully understood by the crowd. The masses don't understand it, yet there it is right in front of them. Truth stands before us in plain view, if we would only take time to notice it. Many times what is hidden remains so only because it is the most noticeable. <u>Familiarity may mask a truth because often what is the most obvious is the most easily overlooked.</u>

The summer crowds remain. I looked forward to the

warm days but certainly not the crowds. In a place like this, I guess that one cannot exist without the other. Out of a need to be alone, I once again desire the coming of winter. Usually I enjoy interaction with others. Now, however, I find that I am more peaceful when alone. My awareness turns toward the environment rather than the people within it. The marine life of the bay seem to sense my desire to be with them. Sea otters, sea lions and dolphins swim nearby, some riding waves with unquestionable confidence. The especially curious ones come in closer to investigate. But they avoid crowds as well. Maybe they seek the reclusive life. Their original natures are probably not far removed from our own. Most of us have slipped far from this original state, so far that we'd barely recognize it if we saw it. As our eyes refocus, another truth slips from view.

Taoist landscape paintings display persons in the background, almost totally hidden from sight. Observing this, we tend to view the practice of Taoism as reclusive. And it's no wonder, seeing persons living deep within the forest, away from society, away from other people, alone with nature. What are we to think when we see a Sung Dynasty landscape painting? Picture an entire mountain with only one barely visible person hidden in the landscape. But the flowing movement of Taoism is progressive, like a mountain stream that begins at the summit, eventually finding its way to the ocean. Taoism is usually never thought of as being progressive because, in a sense, it never strives yet is somehow always successful in gaining new ground.

The cool breeze mixes with the sun's last few warming rays. The sun dips farther toward the ocean once again. Soon the breeze will take over and its cool qualities will be left to give me something more to ponder. The sand seems unaffected by all this as if it is watching from afar. The mood in the air changes with the setting sun. I can no longer concentrate on one thing. Now my mind wanders peacefully, picking up images of my surroundings as I glance around. The tide now is as high as it's going to get this evening. The beach here is wide. Here in this well protected part of the bay, layers of sand have built up and rest unaffected by the small waves that slap onto the shore year around.

The moon is rising and is as full as ever. Sunlight is still just visible over the ridge. I understand why the tide is so high now and realize that there will also be an equally low tide later tonight. As evening falls, the moonlight puts a mysterious glow onto the surface of the waves. The moonlight itself does the dance that demonstrates the flowing movement of Tao. The moonlight is perfect. It is still and motionless and yet moves with ease on the rolling waves, riding each one to shore. This mysterious glow becomes brighter as the hours pass into the night. As the moon rises, the whole ocean becomes aglow with a brilliant radiance. If there were ever a time to night surf, it would be now.

I know that the experience would clear my mind but as I glance over the cliff, I see that the tide is too high and the waves are rolling up against the cliff itself. I walk farther up the point. Each time I look back at the moon, the trail of light is upon me, as if following my every step. The strip of light over the water is narrow, taking on a particular direction.

At the same time it seems to encompass all directions. No matter where I am on the cliff, the trail of light remains with me, and, for a moment, I possess its brilliance.

Each of us has a place where we grew up surfing, or just plain grew up, and that place will forever hold special memories. As children, my friends and I would surf every type of condition presented to us. Among the days of cold wind and choppy surf would be days of glassy, smooth ocean surfaces, and hollow waves. We'd never complain about the surf but would ride whatever came in.

There were those among us who always waited for that perfect day and did nothing but complain in between. They were never pleased, not just with the waves but with life in general. Those who maintained inner peace are very accepting of change toward diverse and even adverse conditions brought about by nature. During heavy rains and huge waves, they observe the change with a smile, knowing that people need to be awakened from their slumber. They feel that every once in a while it is good that nature brings forth a little reminder of our place in its vast scheme. Too often we take the wrong attitude and think we have taken over nature, harnessed it and controlled it. Then something happens to remind us of this unsound and fallacious way of thinking.

That change is imminent can be seen in the land and its people. The places we once surfed as children, the places where we grew up, have all changed. The reefs and sandbars have changed. These places don't break as they used to. Some say that our idea of waves has changed and not the waves themselves, but J disagree. Jt is easy for me to see how the waves no longer break out as far, no longer roll in with the fluidity that they once had. Jt used to sadden me to think of things now in relation to the way they once were. J would think back to the days where even the local beach breaks would create some of the best surf around. For years these days existed as frozen images in my memory. But years later, J found that these phenomenal days do eventually return.

Perhaps J should have expected change when J was young. J knew the coral reefs grew, the sand bars drifted, and the rocks eroded. Each took time and changed at its own rate. The sand bars seemed to shift with each new swell and J thought they always remained. But the great swell of '83 destroyed the existing sand bars of my childhood. Never would this place break the same again. The waves were a playground for us as kids, a place to escape to, a place to learn and reflect. Sometimes J wonder what happened to the old gang, where they are now and what they're doing. Once in a while J'll see someone who still meets with a few of the guys and J'll get the word. J look back, only to see where J've been, but there is never a desire to return. J move forward, cherishing the moment while simultaneously looking ahead, reaching for the future and releasing myself from the past.

Time itself seems to pass in so many ways. J met up with an old friend with whom J grew up. Jt's been three years since we'd last seen one another. Yet when meeting again, I immediately felt that no time had passed, as if we'd been surfing together without interruption since childhood.

On the other hand, when I examine, even for a moment, all that I've experienced in the last three years and beyond, I feel as though I've lived a few life times. Keeping busy seems to expand time — especially during periods of reflection on those times, examining personal growth and self-cultivation. I think it's important to look back into the past but only to see where we've been, to see what has brought us to the place we are now. Yet ultimately, our focus must be on the present. Taoists say, "Take care of today and tomorrow will take care of itself."

After a week of low clouds, which last throughout the day, we finally get a full day of sun. Big waves continue rolling through, but there is none of the stormy weather that usually comes with big waves along this coast. This swell is the biggest of summer. I've seen the sun come out before while the sky retains perfect clarity and the breezes are calming, and have watched the swell also reach a state of perfect quietude. But this swell is stronger and so far, it seems to be holding its force. I don't know how long it will last.

When seeing the Pacific Ocean for the first time, one must feel a sense of awe. I'll never know this. I was born a few blocks from the ocean and have been near it ever since. Traveling from the East and finally hitting that great blue wall of vastness must make one wonder. What must it be like to travel for hundreds of miles of open land and finally be stopped at the edge of the Pacific? For those who are seeing the Pacific for the first time, it might be incredible to see surfers slip so easily from the land into that great body of water. Sliding from one environment into another gives one the sudden realization that the barriers that exist for us are those we place upon ourselves and exist only in the mind.

    I moved north once, and now I feel I must do so again. The journey is different for each person. The last time my journey began west was when the sandbars changed drastically after a great storm. The time to move is now, I thought. I suddenly and abruptly left – without notice. I took to the road and headed north. Now I'm ready to move again, to take to the road once more. I must continue on up the coast. Soon I will begin packing.

    Even though Taoists are not strictly isolationists, I feel a need to continue my journey alone. My home is on the road where everything is in motion, where my only sense of permanence is the very fact of impermanence, permanently moving. I've always known if I stayed in one place very long I'd get that feeling of needing to be back on the road again. While living here, I've made numerous road trips which have provided for me a sense of impermanence, something I've needed in order to survive in one spot for very long. Why do I need mobility when others seem to crave stability? Perhaps when traveling, slipping from place to place, my cherished spontaneity has a greater chance to flourish. But spontaneity is within, not without, for the sage can travel the world without leaving his front yard. Why then do I continue seeking other destinations?

This morning the tide is extremely low and the angle of the swell renders the waves along the point unmakeable. The waves appear to be too fast. The swell pushes the lines around the point and the waves blow toward the inside. This time it seems that a little higher tide could actually be of some help toward shaping the waves. For now, J'll wait. J can always come back another time.

J've got time today to hit the road for a while and explore more of the coast between here and San Francisco. What J'm really interested in is the coastline that stretches north of the Golden Gate. There's a lot of unexplored territory ahead, but this evening, J've chosen to return home to follow the setting sun.

For me, road trips, surfing new breaks, exploring new places fuels the spontaneity of life, stimulates the body, mind, and spirit that becomes renewed and revitalized.

J head on up the coast and pass small towns so characteristic of the coast highway. Heading farther north, the ocean is right outside my window. The sun is out, the morning fog has cleared and the air begins to warm my cold hands. Farmland is on both sides of me and the cliff line varies in height as J drive. Sometimes the road brings me close to the water's edge, close enough to feel the ocean spray. So much open land stretches ahead. My sense of freedom arises not just because J'm on the road but also because of the road J'm on. J feel this road will take me to places where no one has been before, as if it had been here long before our or any other civilization ever was. However, there's something obviously wrong with that and so I examine it no further and choose to rest easily with the pleasant thought. The road stretches endlessly on up the coast. I finally make a roadside stop before San Francisco and pull into a small clearing. As I walk down the path I see a river running through the beach, separating it at one point before emptying into the ocean. The beach is deserted and the waves look smooth and glassy. Over the beach, a hawk hovers in the air current and drifts slowly back and forth keeping me aware of what lies just on the other side of the road; more farmland and land still left in its original state, untouched and uncultivated. Looking farther north, I still see no one. Perfect emptiness.

Before, I might have felt a sense of loneliness, but now I appreciate the relationship I have with the land and sea. Although no one else is here, I no longer feel alone. Nature flourishes here uninhibited. How can I feel alone in this environment where life is so abundant? Human interaction is just around the corner but still far enough away. I suppose I would miss interacting and probably feel the effects of isolation after some time, but civilization never seems out of reach. The offshore breeze wanders down along the hillsides, caressing the fields, finally arriving at the shore and continuing out to sea. Who knows how far the breeze will travel today or where it will travel to? It wanders entirely on its own as if it has some place in mind to go. Or perhaps the breeze is full of spontaneity with no predetermined place in mind. And so it shifts here and wanders there, slowing down, speeding up, and suddenly changing direction once again. The movement is

at times hypnotic and yet its shifting, halting, unpredictable moods keep me alert. I decide that this will be as far north as I will go today, and before long, I head back down.

When I get up the next morning, I see that the swell has weakened and for a moment, the pack thins out. The air is a little cooler today, reminiscent of the coming of winter, when only a few hardy souls will remain to brave the winter swells. It all seems refreshing to me, fewer people in the water, cooler air, and crystal clear skies. Even the air is quieter, which gives me a chance to hear the shore break and the sound of the breeze passing through the pine, cypress and eucalyptus trees, each one delivering a different note, a tune unique unto itself; each one telling me something, revealing truths, reaching into the depths of my soul.

Perhaps I will stay here one more winter before moving on.

Days pass and I try to accomplish too much at once. Forcing things to happen rather than allowing them to come about naturally creates difficulties down the road. Then a point is reached where less gets done no matter how hard I try. There really is an approach to life that is more successful than others. Taoism teaches this Way to be more successful by becoming more relaxed in the approach itself. Maybe it's the focus of effort and a knowing or feeling of how much effort is enough.

I'm suddenly struck by a familiar smell. The swell was powerful enough to pull a lot of kelp free from the bottom. The high tide delivered the piles onto the beach sometime in

the night. Now the midday sun dries the lifeless bunches
and I watch them disintegrate before me.

Some kelp still sits offshore, tangled, twisted and moving about by the will of the current and small waves that
remain from remnants of the past swell. Overhead, the air is
warmer today and a faint but distinct ring encircles the sun.
I'm not sure what causes it or what it all means. I don't know
the significance yet, but in time I know it will come to me.

With so many tourists and fair-weather surfers around
I draw back farther and farther into myself. The longer I
stay here, the more removed I become from everything
around me. But when I'm on the road heading out of town,
there's a sudden release, like I've broken through a barrier
that has kept me locked in too long. I release myself from
the dark chambers within the recesses of my soul. As I
head out, the radio becomes useless noise, further disrupt-
ing the pattern of my brain waves and so I quickly turn it
off. Each of my breaths pace themselves, my mind intent on
clarity, yearning once again to return to my natural state,
and wonder exactly what that means.

I pass a three-digit town, reminiscent of fifty or more
years ago. All these small towns that run along this highway were populated with less than a thousand, some only a
few hundred at best. To see that only a couple hundred make
up this town is peaceful to me. For a moment I forget the
year, I forget all the modern technology and the big city
noise. I left it behind, some place way back. I no longer

remember quite where. It doesn't matter to me now. For now, I'm on the road, and that's what matters.

With perfect symmetry and form, a lone tractor heads out across the land, all the way out until the land is no more. It's morning now, and the wind is offshore. The waves continue to roll through in front of these fields as they have done for generations before. Without a care, the tractor continues over the land, its tires pressing a unique pattern into the dark soil with each revolution like the lines that form on the faces of those who cultivate the land itself.

When it rains, I stand along the cliff and hear the water fall onto the crops while the waves crash below. As the wind calms I sense the stillness in the air. These are the light and fragrant rains, characteristic to the season and this particular region.

The sky now begins to clear, with patches of blue and white. As the clouds pass overhead, the shadows wander about the hillsides like a shadow dance that mesmerizes and leaves one wondering what patterns will appear next.

Wind drifts over the hills. The lines moving across the fields resemble the swell lines that enter the bay after a great wind somewhere off the coast. Nature's patterns are revealed everywhere. If we'd only take time to notice, then we'd see identical patterns appearing in places we'd never expected.

This morning was clear. These last few weeks, the early morning fog settled in until nearly noon. As the sun appeared from behind the hill, rays of light dispersed through the gentle mist that settles in the forest overnight. I wanted to capture

this moment on film, but realized that I could never capture
what I was now seeing. Somehow, the lens separated me
from the reality, the moment, the event as it was happening.
A quality photograph is marked by the photographer's ability
to capture the moment as we might experience it ourselves.
To these photographers, the world is viewed through a cam-
era lens but they are not separated from the objects they
view. If anything, the objects become more real and vivid
than what the naked eye can apprehend. Once in a while
we will see a photograph that moves us emotionally. In some
way we relate to the photograph. It might be something
that stirs the memory of long ago, conjuring up images, images that make us pause for a moment and reflect. The
power of the photograph lies in its ability to move us; com-
mencing action, movement, and introspection.

The sun's rays separate individually and cast themselves down upon the tranquil waters of the bay. What is
interesting about watching a sunrise is noting all the immediate changes in its continuous movement. Midday is not so
easy, not so noticeable. In the early morning hours, I can
look at the sun while it still appears as a faint glow before it
becomes too bright to observe with the naked eye.

The swell has picked up again without a moment's rest
after the last one. I'm not sure how the tide will affect the
waves, but as I sit out here, waiting for the next set, I notice that something is different with each wave I ride. The
tide was coming up earlier this morning. The low tide caused
impossible sections. Now the rides are short and quick which
sharpens my reflexes and keeps me alert. As the tide rises
the waves begin to open up. The rides are longer, not quite

as fast but becoming workable all the way down the line.
The peak shifts over a bit to another spot on the reef. J
drop in farther and farther back with each wave. J line myself
up with a pipe that runs down the side of the cliff and go
from there. At low tide there would be no way of making the
wave from behind the pipe. Now every wave J drop into is
from the back. Out here everything is changing, constantly
moving without interference. J sit and observe, but quickly
come to understand that, out here, observation alone is not
possible without simultaneously becoming an active partici-
pant. The subject-object relationship is somehow intertwined,
intermeshed, linked like the waves and the ocean, each one
a part of the other, each a part of the great whole.

    The sun becomes more intense as we approach Au-
gust. Jts rays go right through me now, and penetrate to
the core of my soul, to the innermost reaches of my body, my
very existence. Looking across the beach, J see the waves
rising out of the sand from the intense heat. The sand gets
hotter by the minute. Everything here is so far removed from
the cool mist covered forest J remember. J'm in another
time and place. Sweat trickles down my face, it too finding
its own path. A gentle mist would feel good now. The ocean
draws me closer. J feel that if J stay on the beach any longer,
J'll slowly melt and disappear between the infinite grains of
sand that all fit so neatly together, like a puzzle that moves
but never comes apart. J hesitate no longer. Maybe J never
hesitated at all, and find myself alone in the cool shorebreak —

naked and free from all the inhibitions that prevented my escape from a cell of lonely solitude, where my only interaction was with myself. Only I can set myself free. My focus has been redirected. If there were ever any hesitation, it exists no longer. I yearn for interaction, but it is no longer the interaction with others that I yearn for. This is why I now stand here alone with the waves that have traveled for thousands of miles, to finally rest upon these beaches, to sink into these structureless layers of sand. Alone, but not lonely, never lonely . . . and I guess never really alone.

Chapter Two

Dialogues of Plato, The Phaedo

Well then, as J said at the beginning, if a man
has trained himself through his life to live in a state
as close as possible to death, would it not be
ridiculous for him to be distressed when death comes?

— Socrates

We were both strong swimmers from all the years of surfing. As ocean swimmers, we emphasized strength rather than speed. We had endurance for the long haul. Jf we lost our surfboard while on the outer reef, we would need every bit of endurance and strength to swim through the waves and currents. J always thought of my brother as a faster swimmer but we ended up using each other as pace-setters.

J was always amazed at the way he rode big waves, fearless and with confidence. The waves he rode became a part of him, as he became a part of the waves. There seemed to be no separation between the two. His fluid style emphasized that. Since he was older, J looked to him for knowledge, experiential knowledge that comes with time, with age.

He knew where the waves came from, why the wind blew in the direction it did. We'd stand together along the cliff in the chill of the early morning. Gazing out to sea, he'd study the waves, the intervals, the way they broke across the reef. He was calm, watchful and contemplative. He possessed the inner qualities I needed to develop in myself. After studying the waves, we'd head down the trail into the desolate cove. He'd already know when to paddle out. He knew where the channels were, which way the current was running and the height of the tide, all of which become more critical as the waves increase in size.

In the early years, we'd travel south to a reef break near San Diego. We'd arrive before dawn. The chill from the morning air challenged us to change into our wetsuits as quickly as possible. I remember the grass shack, a place we'd leave our surfboards while sitting next to the fire, waiting for the trickle of light to penetrate our childlike euphoria, unleashing exuberance and energy beyond command. Without further ado, we'd suit up and head out to ride once more.

As I looked back to each day that passed, it seemed like long ago, and yet I would always remember it as if it were yesterday. I recalled the events that stood out as milestones. There were days when many of us from the old gang would ride together, and although those days were spectacular, they were rare. More often, I'd ride with my brother at places he knew were isolated, with no one to be seen for miles around. This is how I knew him. As we got older, our visits became less frequent, but somehow we were still able to take time out to ride waves together. Surfing would always be necessary. I always arrived at his place when he knew there would be traces of a new swell. Our timing had always been impeccable. What would come of the visit this time would change our lives forever.

Pulling up to the old house along the canals in Long Beach, there was my brother, packing up to move to New Mexico to be near our sister. Why the sudden rush to head out of California? He pulled me aside saying, "Here, take these boards, I want you to have them." I knew that a surfer only gives up his boards if he knows he'll never be surfing again, at least not in the waves as we know them in this world. My only response was that I'd hold on to them until we could ride again. He didn't say anything. It was then that I realized that there was more to this than was immediately in my grasp. I told him that I'd contact him in New Mexico to check up on things. But New Mexico, why would a big wave rider head toward the Southwest? These questions lingered with me. Possible answers came without acknowledging them. What confronted me in the following week would deliver me on a journey into the unknown to face the innermost reaches of the Self.

My brother now waits for his arrival in a new place, crossing the barriers into another realm. I'm alerted as to his condition and know that I cannot wait another moment to see him. J need to be by his side as he was for me on those days we'd ride together.

J call my sister. She informs me of his current state, that he decided to stop taking the AJDS medicine and all medicine, even those that were preventing the spread of pneumonia. She said he wouldn't last until the end of the week. He was never the type to give up, but J knew this time he had enough.

J felt that he was waiting to pass on into another world until J got there. Oddly enough, J had spoken with him on Monday. He was able to talk and said he was looking forward to me coming out. J told him then that J would check on air fares and get back with him. By Friday, they said he might not make it through the night. When J called this morning, he was sleeping but still alive. J wasted no time this morning in getting a flight out immediately. Southwest airlines to El Paso. J'd be picked up in El Paso and driven to Las Cruces, New Mexico — about an hour from the airport. J keep saying to myself — hold on — hoping he can hear me. Hold on, J'm on my way, hoping he knows, believing that he does, becoming impatient, wanting to be there now to watch over him.

Early in the week, my sister said he didn't have much longer. J didn't know at the time how to interpret this. J wanted, of course, to believe this meant — maybe a couple of years as opposed to a life time. He's in his thirties. After talking with her, she said he's not going to make it through the following week. J was suddenly confronted with a painful realization, that this once hardy young surfer was not going to be with us much longer. J wanted to believe that he would still be with us and understood that to believe is more comforting than to not believe. J have no evidence, no empirical data to support my belief, but let this one unsubstantiated belief rest quietly, away from the opposition and refutations.

Flying over Yosemite

Leaving on this flight was difficult because the flight forced me to confront reality. At first J had trouble making the reservations, thinking that he really was going to be fine and that J need not be so quick to fly out — for flying out on a moment's notice would indicate seriousness, something J had a difficult time facing. The reality of it won out and here J am on a plane to El Paso. J feel that J need to be there tonight in case he doesn't make it through to the morning. J couldn't wait another night at home. There again, J know it would be like last night — dreaming of my brother through the night, waking up at all hours, wondering when morning would come, worried to call and see if he made it through to the next day. But as it got later in the evening, J thought that maybe J'd see him, that he'd come to visit me before he left if he couldn't make it through to the next day, if he couldn't wait for me to get there. These thoughts lingered with me throughout the night.

Phoenix, AZ, 8:25 ready for take off. Push the clock ahead one hour for Texas.

On the way up again — to 25,000 feet. Palms sweat a bit, J'd rather be on the ground, on a train, where J can feel the land beneath my feet through the steel rails. The stewardess has a cute Texan accent. Como Tejas no hey otro!

Reading a bit. The sun hits me – directly into my face, blinding me suddenly for a moment. I push the shade up to block out the light. I try and relax but it's not that easy. I don't know if the cabin is getting warm or if it's just me.

Two hour flight from Phoenix – an hour drive from El Paso into New Mexico – quick – but I'd travel by train again at the drop of a hat. I feel that he's holding on. I visualize myself talking with him and him understanding me, not losing any of his abilities to comprehend.

The cabin feels cooler now – for a moment. I called from Phoenix to let them know I was on my way. When I get back, I should keep his surfboard inside to hang on the wall, protected. But I wonder if he would rather I continue riding it as he would have. I'm not sure – but I am sure that now is not the time to decide such things either way. I shall attend to that later when my head is clearer, not that it isn't clear now, but perhaps I mean when some things are sorted through more thoroughly, then the answers will come as they always have in the past. Let the mind flow and the problem solving creative side will have a much better chance to do its job – and do it well.

One of the stewardesses spots me writing and turns on the overhead light for me before I can say anything about it. These are the angels who roam the earth!

Thursday, the 9th

J arrive late in the evening and greet him in his relaxed, semi- conscious state. He's been sleeping but is fully
aware that J am now with him. J sit for a while beside him,
trying to respond to him the best J can. J speak little. That
we are here together speaks for itself. J let him know that
he can fall back to sleep, that we can continue our conver-
sation in the morning. J assure him that he'll be all right.

Friday, the 10th

He made it through another night. And now another
day is presented to us — minutes pass and we notice the
existence of each. J sit with him, J don't know how long —
it doesn't matter. He holds my hand and J return the grip.
He seems to find a sense of security in my being here. J talk
with him about returning to the beach, a place where he can
once again find peace and comfort. J tell him that the beach
is his home away from it all — his real home. J conjure up
delightful images of the beach so that maybe they can wander through his mind; the warm breeze, the smell of coconut
surf wax, the taste of the salt, the feel of the sand and the
warmth of the sun as a new day begins. J use Taoist metaphors of surfing to let him know that the unknown (death) is
nothing to fear, for he had known no fear before when ven-
turing into new surf spots — when dropping into the biggest
waves. He has conquered all. J remind him that riding big
waves in storm conditions is the greatest feat of all and that
nothing else could take such great endurance. J explore the

tube-ride as the metaphor for passing from one world into another, but never use the word "death' or "dying."

He seems to be more at peace when I continue to talk
to him about surfing — and remind him that, in some way,
we'll all surf together again — telling him that I'll meet him
out in the lineup.

I want to bring back to him the surfing mind-set, so
that he can pass on, fearless, as he was in the water.

The front door suddenly opened, but no one was there,
the wind outside doesn't seem strong enough to open doors.
I remain calm and receptive to new phenomena.

I want him to pass on with dignity. He's lost a lot of
weight — and is bedridden. He can only get out of bed if we
help him. He was a once strong and powerful surfer — and
I shall always remember him that way — as will we all.

6:19 p.m.

I sit here in the room with him and write. I remind
him of the day and time. I realize that I lost track of the
days when I was touring the U.S. by train. Mom calls to
see how things are and to my surprise, my brother picks up
the phone and begins speaking to her with the little energy
he has left. He seems to be going in and out of a dream
state, waking now and then. This time he wakes saying that
he's just seen something in the room near me.

10:09 p.m.

I'm not sure if it's delusions or simply a dream state and

perhaps slight disorientation. Nevertheless, he is aware that he is experiencing periods of disorientation. Despite the illness, J see him continue to emphasize his higher states of reason.

J slept pretty well last night – better than J had a few days earlier at home. Now J am here with him, no longer wondering about what's happening a thousand miles away, but right here, where J can be with him when he decides to pass on to the other side.

Usually Angels have appeared before me during times of hardship – but this time, oddly enough, J've been treated like J am the Angel who has appeared, arriving when J was needed most, for moral support – and to share some comforting philosophy on life, death and the transition between.

10:42 p.m.

J went in to say good-night. He thanked me for coming, and said that J made a difference by being here with him. That's all J needed to hear to make the trip more meaningful and in some way helpful to all – nothing more can be said.

J'm preparing now to sleep for the evening. My perspective on death has changed. Perhaps J'm more relaxed now than ever before; walking my brother through this passage gives me a new understanding. Being close to him allows me to see more clearly the nature of things in the here and now, with pure spontaneity, living in the moment, being there close and facing it.

Saturday, the 11th, 8:09 a.m.

He has chosen to be with us another day — but I think
in someway, he'll always be near. He will remain as a powerful memory. Perhaps, in this way, his presence will never
leave us.

His funny sense of humor is still with him. He complains
now at the sound of the trucks that drive behind the house,
just as he complained about the sirens that plagued his Long
Beach home. I laugh to see that he has not changed.

9:01 a.m.

Just before I arrived here on Saturday, I was alerted
that he made one suicide attempt. I do not think it had anything to do with depression. Rather he was simply tired of
living in his current condition. I know that he's already gone
farther than he wanted to in the first place. No one wants to
wait to the point where they cannot get out of bed by themselves. He was strong, independent and self-sufficient. We shall
do everything in our power to help preserve his dignity.

This afternoon my sister and a worker from the hospice
are coming over to evaluate the situation. I sit here now in a
chair next to my brother's bed and continue to write.

10:09 a.m.

Writing is helping me to hold things together by letting
thoughts and feelings flow out onto paper. A warm wind
blows outside — through the window I see the leaves and

small branches move gracefully and naturally around the flickering sunlight.

I weighed myself last night. I see that I'm 179 lbs., which surprises me. I thought I was closer to 185. I don't look skinny — just defined from the hard workouts surfing along the point. I realize though that I haven't really eaten very much in the last few days. Dinner was good and I'm sure it brought me back over 180 pounds. We had dinner at our sister's house. Shrimp and cheese enchiladas and a homemade sauce to cover the corn tortillas. It's the first real meal I've had in about a week.

9:01 p.m.

Earlier today I went for a quick run down the dirt road that winds its way through the cotton fields, which right now are simply fields of tractor-plowed dirt. I can feel the difference in elevation. It's about 4,300 feet here. I run, shirt off, shorts on and wearing boots. The two dogs run with me and sometimes ahead of me.

We talked to him today about how he wanted to be buried. I told him I could put his ashes in the waves.

Sunday, the 12th, 9:02 a.m.

He's resting after breakfast. I asked him again about spreading his ashes in the waves. I mentioned the Bay and told him that it was a National Marine Preserve. I told him that the water was clear, beautiful and untouched by man —

that the otters, seals, and dolphins thrived. I said, for me, I wanted my ashes to be thrown into the waves, so that I could gently flow with the current and the tides, so that I could end up on some of the beaches in the warmth of the sand. This all appealed to him greatly — and so on this day, I plan to carry out his wish — I'll put him in the crystal blue waters of the bay, to drift peacefully with the ever changing tides.

A friend of ours called. He's the tribal elder, someone we have both surfed with for years. He said he was going down to San Clemente to paddle out and get a wave for my brother. He said he'd ride it like he's never done before.

Those who can't be here do what they must to appease the surf gods and their own state of mind. None of us can rest until we each do something to pay our last respects — and I already know the psychological benefit from this will be enormous.

For me, I know I could not stand another day going by without being here with him.

9:38 a.m.

I am more at peace being here, knowing exactly what's going on — even though being here is difficult, some times more difficult than others. Still, I'd not have it any other way.

11:25 a.m.

The Catholic priest just came by to perform the last

rites for him. He was not here more than ten minutes. Now
I sit here in front of the house — on the porch — facing the
Organ Mountains. It's eighty in the shade — the warm
breeze gently passes through the porch.

The Father's visit did not seem very personal. It seemed
more like a job, but I guess that is his job. The social worker
and the R.N. were much more hospitable — warmer — and
seemed to be more caring; but this is their job too, and their
jobs allowed them to spend more time here.

The R.N. from the hospice said that she does not support the idea of anyone "harming" themselves. She does not
advocate intervention toward the desired goal of death. She
will, however, intervene to the point of keeping down the
pain. I don't know if she has to say this for legal reasons or
if she actually believes this — because if this is what she
believes, I think it ludicrous. She is very well aware that in
the next week, he may neither desire nor be able to take any
more food or liquids. My immediate thought was that I would
certainly not stand by and watch him get any weaker, any
thinner, or any sicker. While he's still very coherent, I will
honor his wishes — and if he desires to end this life, I will
not prevent it.

4:51 p.m.

I again return to the porch to get fresh air and see the
shadows dance upon the rocks from the sunlight passing
through the small plants that continue to flourish in this dry
region.

The warm breeze now blows toward me for a moment,

directly into my face. For some reason I think of Hawaii and its warm, tropical breezes. It's actually cooler when the wind comes up, because even in the brief moment that the wind dies, I can feel a sudden rise in temperature. The wind adds movement which somehow is comforting to me. I walk over to a grove of trees and hear the call of various birds, which I cannot identify until I spot a quail perched on an outer limb.

Monday, 10:05 p.m.

I've realized my dreams are clearer and I remember them in detail now that I'm here. Last week my dreams were more chaotic — running together like a thousand thoughts. When I attempted to transfer them onto paper, I found the task nearly impossible.

10:26 p.m.

We went out for Japanese food tonight. I return home and glance into a mirror. At first I am merely a silhouette in the moon until I turn on some light. I see the beard that has grown since my arrival on Saturday. Some of the whiskers are grey, the rest of my beard is dark, leaving a shadow visible from far away.

The wind outside has slowed to a very calm breeze, and at nearly 11:00 at night it feels like it's eighty degrees.

I'll be flying out tomorrow afternoon, instinctively knowing that he'll still be with me, that he will have passed on before the weekend comes. He's decided that it's time. He's very tired and even looks like he has only hours left. He wants to slip into a deep sleep, to never again awake.

It's somewhere between 1:30 a.m. and 2:00 — I hear him calling all the way from the back of the house — I get up and respond as quickly as I can. He asks for some iced tea and complains of being terribly thirsty. I feel the same way. The air in the house is still very warm despite the fact that we've left some windows open.

I hear the whistle blow from the train. It sounds very familiar to me after my Amtrak trip only a month ago. It sounds like it could be the same line I was on, coming through New Mexico into El Paso, Texas.

He drinks the iced tea I made for him, a mixture of orange and mint at his request. He wants me to clear off his side table and put a piece of glass over it. This piece was specially cut for the unusual shape some years before but was simply not put on since the move. Not yet 2:00 in the morning — an unusual request for me to hear at this late hour, but not unusual for him under the circumstances. I feel he is still thinking of some last minute things to take care of before he goes, and so I not only understand his request but also honor it.

Now I sit in a chair beside his bed. He's fallen back asleep now. Two small room lights are on. The time function flashes on the VCR. The sound of an occasional truck is audible on the highway near the mountains. Things are suddenly very quiet. My pen touching the paper seems loud, so I write slowly. I can hear him breathing, not because his breathing is loud, but simply because the air is so still.

A little after . . . he wakes up suddenly while I am writing. I never complete the sentence. He's thirsty again. He doesn't know I'm still in the room with him and tries to reach over and get the glass of iced tea without calling one of us again. I sense that he feels bad having to constantly call us to take care of things for him.

I talk with him, now a little past 2:00 in the morning and help him with the glass. He's finally got a firm grip on it and insists on holding it himself. The ice cubes have melted but the liquid, and for that matter, even the glass itself is still cold to the touch. I'm sure the cold glass feels good to him as heat from his body transfers to the glass. The exchange is doing him some good.

He thanks me and says how he's truly going to miss me.

A sudden gust of wind appears in the front of the house and then disappears as quickly as it came.

The train comes by again. This one can't be Amtrak. It's only an hour later. Only one Amtrak train a day runs through here. But still the whistle sounds familiar, probably because there is a certain sound and certain length of time that the whistle must be blown when going through populated areas.

Almost three in the morning. I'm not sure if I should just try to stay here and fall asleep in the chair next to him, or go back to my own bed for a bit.

3:00 a.m.

He calls my name. I go over to his bedside. He says he's just been dreaming but seems too tired right now to tell me about it. I ask him anyway and he just says something indicating that he realizes the nonsensical nature of the dream. He is still able to make a sharp distinction between dream state and being awake. I consider each to be a form of reality.

The trucks pound the highway just outside. I don't think I'll have any trouble leaving this afternoon knowing that he'll be traveling to new places sometime tonight, and knowing too that I'll be sprinkling his ashes in the waves soon. To me, the event will not be a separation but rather a reunification.

3:12 a.m.

I try falling asleep in this wooden chair, sitting up. I'm aware of his every breath, every movement. I can't really fall asleep being this alert. Or maybe I can if I relax enough. The eighteen wheelers again pound their tires on the pavement, sending the sounds through the small opening in the window left open for fresh air to flow through during the night.

4:00 a.m.

He wakes up again — feeling thirsty. I give him the last of the iced tea by his bedside. He requests more and asks for more sugar this time. I go back to the kitchen and refill his glass, add more sugar and ice cubes. The fluids feel good to him and I feel good assisting him to make things a little more pleasant in his final hours.

I will try to stay by his bedside in this wooden chair

until I can see light outside. Then I'll try and get a little extra sleep myself.

4:11 a.m.

Again I know I've grown from this experience. I know too that as each day passed since my arrival, I've in some ways become stronger. I simply feel good knowing that I'm helping to make things a little more comfortable for him. I rest with the thought that his tired body, which serves as a temporary shell, will no longer be needed and that the rest of him in some way lives on.

At 4:30 I decide to go back to my bed. The carved wood in the chair is sticking me in the back. He seems like he'll be fine 'til sunup.

I wake at various intervals throughout the night. Now at 6:30 a.m., I sit up in bed.

9:26 a.m.

I'm a little hungry now and get a carton of yogurt out of the refrigerator. I sit on the porch once again. The sun is getting higher in the sky. It seems extremely quiet. I'm not used to it yet. When I'm at home, at the very minimum, I hear waves breaking or the fog horn coming from the harbor entrance.

Birds sing. I hear the quail that I was listening to yesterday and expect that she is in the same place, a place high in the tree tops. Other birds sound off, but I'm not sure what types they all are. The thermometer reads 70 degrees in the shade. The sun hits my legs under the patio roof. It feels like it's going to be another very warm day.

9:37 a.m.

The R.N. from the hospice pulls up. I walk toward her and tell her that he's not doing well at all.

She leaves after a short period and says if we need anything to give her a call.

Now at a quarter to eleven it's nearly eighty in the shade. I remind my brother how he introduced me to a lot of classical music, hoping he'll want to hear some. I think it will help the mood — set the stage for his transference. It works and he requests the Sibelius Symphonies 1 & 6. I put in the disc and let it play. I am struck with images of his old apartment where he first introduced this music to me.

11:00 a.m.

I sit here now beside him. The clock is ticking. He seems tired, but relaxed and ready for the transformation. It feels good to be here beside him. He rests quietly while listening to the music coming from the living room. He moves a little, his legs move back and forth and then come to a rest. He has fallen asleep, and this time, he will not again awake.

The two dogs lay beside each other at the foot of the bed, mother and daughter. I wonder how much they know.

6:53 p.m. In flight to San Francisco

As I sit here, I realize that I'm not the same person who left home only four days ago. My mind reflects on the last day.

A baby is laid down on the seat across from me. Her parents change her diaper. She's smiling — a very happy baby. A new life into this world.

Tuesday, the 14th

Back home once again. I finally got in around eleven last night. I slept for a few hours this afternoon. Wound up, I didn't get to sleep until nearly 1:00 this morning — then got up at 5:30 to get some waves.

I reached for my brother's surf board, and again wondered about riding it. I thought that perhaps this day would be the last time this board should be in the waves. I knew I'd get some impressive waves — and we did. Strange too, other surfers were saying how during the week, the waves had been small, but this morning everything was going. I paddled out with some new strength, some type of invincibility that I've never known before. I knew that my perception and thoughts concerning death had changed since I last left here only a week earlier.

The clouds sat low along the hills and the sun rose slowly from behind the bay. The red glow appeared under the clouds before the sun came over the ridge. There was a peacefulness here that I had never felt anywhere else. I knew this was the place for my brother to be buried, out here in the midst of all the fantastic splendor and natural beauty that only the bay can present.

Now I feel the effects from the ordeal I endured last week. My feelings shift suddenly from sadness to happiness and then anger. I realize that what I went through last week will have long-lasting effects.

I am less fearful of death than ever before, and for some reason, I now seek it out. I want to show that I have no fear, to prove something to myself.

So many thoughts run through my head. I find it difficult to write, or to know exactly what to write.

I'm finally eating again, something more substantial, turkey meat and a salad. I don't feel that I've completely caught up on my sleep yet, perhaps the ordeal has taken its toll. I feel tired still — of course, staying up until midnight and getting up at 5:00 in the morning to surf hasn't helped my recovery.

An 8" x 10" photo of the gang at San Onofre sits here in the kitchen, visible from every angle.

In some way I hope to see him, or feel his presence in a way greater than memory alone can bring.

I've sent out notification letters to all of us who rode together, letting them know of the events that have transpired.

I can divert my attention, but then I fail to deal with all that has gone on. Writing helps, surfing is also beneficial. Eating well and of course getting enough sleep add to the recovery – but the main issues need to be verbalized.

Images continue to appear in my mind. Seeing him as I sat there beside him, as he rested in a chair. With my hand on his shoulder, leaning his head over, and with the little strength he had left, he rests his cheek against my hand, like saying, thanks for being here, thanks for being by my side as I exit this world and enter another. You're someone special to me, someone I was able to be brothers with. Then as he raised his head again, I put my hand on his head, and combed his hair back with my fingers, gently caressing him, looking at him, looking at him slowly fade, trying not to fall apart, trying to give him all my strength, holding back my tears, not always being successful, but still trying nevertheless. Watching his every movement. I sensed he knew what I'm going through, watching him, being by his side during all this, for a moment came when he looked over at me, but remained expressionless, fearless, and painless, slowly drifting, drifting, drifting.

I remember family looking on, tears flowing without any concern, pure and free, spontaneous, powerful, emotional, uninhibited, expressive, and embracing – of all the moments that we've shared, the moments in time that stand still, motionless, lasting now for eternity.

I think of my brother each day now. A day has not passed that the image of him does not enter my thoughts.

I now can not sleep without having continuous dreams

throughout the night. The trauma has caught up with me. I now realize the true power of the event. Perhaps I did my best to hold back my own emotions to be strong for others who needed the support. But now I feel the effects. For unknown reasons I sometimes seek confrontation, perhaps a form of misdirected anger. I am exhausted. The anxiety is bringing about many dreams. My sleep is not restful. I always seem to need more. I am sleepy even as I write.

As the fear of death is the demon that is passed on from one generation to the next, one must do battle and conquer it to prevent it from being passed on to our sons and daughters. Never before was death fearful to me. But now I have taken this demon from him so that he could pass on peacefully and fearlessly. Now I must face death again. This time it is my own.

Perhaps my anger stems from the feeling of helplessness. It is in my character to always take action and have control of things. But the Taoists flow with what cannot be changed. I still have so far to go.

I'm usually in so much control of my life, but here I could do nothing to save him — nothing.

What would happen if you could look death right in the face, fearlessly? I realized that death was, as the Chinese believe, a demon, but only a demon if it haunts you, if you are fearful of it. It seemed that I took it upon myself to take this demon away from him, so that he could die a peaceful death, without fear. But I eventually realize that the demon itself is not death but the fear that arises from death, from the fear of the unknown.

I remember that part of our conversations were about

his fears of passing on to the other side. I wanted so desperately to be a great strength to him in his final hours, so much so that I chose unconsciously to capture this demon so that he could rest peacefully. Capturing the demon meant releasing him from his fears of death. Pulling him away from his fears pushed me into the face of death, something over which I soon had no choice.

In doing so, a great turmoil inside myself boiled, having to deal with this demon I had now captured. I now possessed the fear that went along with facing death itself. With the fear came anger, anger stemming from not having control over something. For years I've placed great emphasis on having total control over myself, my emotions, my thoughts, and my strengths. Now I felt I had suddenly lost a part of my control, and was embedded in a kind of helplessness and despair, a helplessness that I felt when I first saw him upon my arrival. But I overcame the helplessness by finally ridding him of his fears, even if it meant that I would now take these demons upon myself to deal with later. No doubt all of these things caused me to dream — to dream late last night.

In my dream, I found myself in a place where death itself was present, and I was alone, alone to face the demon that was bringing about my inner turmoil. Death was not represented as a particular form, but I knew very clearly that death was there. It was time for me to face this demon and put an end to my inner turmoil. Ultimately, I stayed to face death. I knew that if I was able to stay close to the demon without any harm coming to me, that I would have conquered death and could walk away victor.

It makes sense that I would do anything I could for my brother to help make his transformation peaceful, fearless, and tranquil. I remember saying, "It feels good knowing that I'm helping to make things more pleasant for him." It would disturb me to such a degree to see my brother fearful of death that I would take the fear from him, knowing that I was stronger and more in a position to conquer this fear. How the transference is made, where one takes it upon himself to accept the fears of others, I don't yet know.

I awoke this morning feeling energetic, knowing that during the night, I had battled with death and conquered my fear of it by ultimately defeating it. The turmoil had ended, and my peaceful nature was once again restored.

For the first time after the dream, I was able to wake with energy, unlike the countless days before where I awoke exhausted. Waking in this fashion made me realize to the extent to which conquering this demon was at the root of all my previous days of fluctuating feelings, violent thoughts, and loss of sleep. My spirit had no choice but to do battle with the demon — and ultimately defeat it — or I would live in a continuously troubled state, not knowing what to expect with each passing day.

Now I find myself again traversing the highway leading to euphoria, taking matters into my own hands, distancing myself from illusion, acting, not reacting, rebelling from seemingly inescapable norms that demarcate good from evil during the interludes of fall. Masses pulling through into two lanes coming over the hill, fanatical, repressive, exhausting. Eluding the city I head for the forest covered hills to view the bay under a different light, a second viewing, a second reading, pulling in the lost fragments hidden between the lines, the endless lines that wrap into the bay, untouched, unaided, except by the energy from within.

Penetrating the reef, soaking up images from the tide pools of my mind, shadows dance effortlessly upon the interior walls, a spectrum of evolutionary ideas spring from the well of knowledge. I try desperately to recall the images, but immediately fail in the presence of my consciousness, the Self that stands so close. The images have become shuffled through the deck, like a lost card that eventually finds its way farther and farther down the pile. I try to become of one mind without fluctuating thoughts, but find it impossible to achieve. The different places I travel to, even different settings create many worlds for me, many realities. I become consumed in each, until I head out to a new destination. I blast out of one only to become immersed into another immediately following my sudden absence from the first. Separate realities in different states of Being. Fluctuating like a pendulum, I'm able to finally break free from the distractions clouding my thoughts.

Chapter Three

Tao Te Ching

Water is at once the most yielding of elements
and the mightiest of eroding forces.

— Lao Tzu

J have arrived safely once again on the central coast and have left the aftermath of trauma and confusion behind. Now my ride is with the wind and the wind is at my back, pushing me forward, accelerating me without effort. The moon rises. Because the air is so clear, craters are noticeable in the fullness of its Being. J feel that J can reach out and grasp it, pull it towards me and hold it close and watch the lunar transformation from where J stand. J realize that change will only be noticeable from afar and so let it go, like so many other things before, let it go to follow its own path. The sun is dropping fast as J head north through the rose colored glare bouncing off my starry, penetrating eyes. The hills roll with gracefulness all their own. The clarity seems intensified, for now even the limbs of trees that are scattered about are distinct among the surrounding stalks. The hills become timeless, black silhouettes as the sun disappears behind them. Only a faint outline is noticeable and even this begins to disintegrate before me. Huge bodies of steel ride past me in the night, lights aglow. I continue on up through the farms, through the lush, darkened fields, never passing without appreciating the sweat that has dripped into this soil from the brows of workers cultivating this land. I swerve to the right as each of the eighteen wheelers passes me as I travel around the bay, surfboards on top glide with me through the night. Darkness reveals what daylight fears to expose. I drift into the night, into the vast expanses of space I now feel as the wheels beneath me roll onward.

Being on the road for so long, I'm now merely an extension of it, interacting with the layers of asphalt. I blast through the heat rising from this porous invention. Bridges become symbolic of what leads me to the other side. I can't find my way to the other side without it. But what the other side is symbolic of is yet to be revealed.

Again, I pass persons on the highway that don't seem to know where they're going and yet are still in a hurry to get there. I know these people aren't thinking, and that's sad. They have the ability to be mindful yet remain in an altered state. They're unaccepting of the realities of the road. The difference between myself and them is that I take my time on this road. I've got no place in mind to go and all the time in the world to get there. Some are in a hurry to get somewhere and have in mind where they're going. Its even worse to be in a hurry and not know where you are going.

I've chosen to leave the road open, realizing that the road itself places no limits on how far or where I can go. The distance and places to which I travel are purely dependent upon my will. The road ends where I want it to. I continue towards my unknown destination.

I leave one foot planted on the ground, but let the other take me places, places I've never been before. Living in reality, I can still dream, still wonder, and can find peacefulness and solitude in the late night hours, where the untold future begins unfolding before my eyes. I set out on my journey. Somehow, there is truth on this road, truth that reveals itself without my grasping for it. It comes to me without desire, without force, without apprehension like the lines on the road that speed towards me. Truth stays with me, standing the test of time. Eternal and ancient, it moves on without a care.

A new day. Family has gathered here along the bay. Today, we will bury him at sea as he had requested in his final hours. I was not certain exactly where I would pour his ashes into the ocean. He wanted to be buried in the crystal clear protected waters of the bay, but we never spoke of a specific place. A half hour before the ceremony at the Catholic mission, I located a private cove perfect for this occasion. The air was cool and still, the sky overcast, and the water, a clear emerald green. I set the surfboard he rode so majestically onto the white sands of this small beach. Every action was becoming a symbolic part of the ceremony itself. Even putting the wax on the board was done with care. I tied the container holding his ashes around my waist, along with the roses, and my pack full of purple bougainvillea blossoms. My full wet suit on, feet bared, and everything in place, I entered the water. I could feel the delicate grains of sand so characteristic to this part of the bay. The water's clarity allowed me to see the impressions in the sand, the same lines characterized by wind upon sand dunes. I began paddling, not knowing where I would end up. I noticed patches of kelp sitting nearly a hundred yards offshore and stopped just before reaching them. I gazed for a moment into the distance. The ocean stretched out until I could see no more. The kelp continuously moved with the swells as they entered this protected cove. Undoing the container, I released the ashes into the water beside me, slowly, uniformly, watching as each grain mixed with the sea. As the ashes and water mixed, a cloud formed, resembling a plume of dust in the air.

Nothing was planned, everything was totally spontaneous. I didn't know what I was going to do from one minute to the next, almost in a trance, except everything was done willfully. I kept going, already becoming tired from the exertion and the stress, the emotion and the willingness to push on. Before the weekend came to a close, my body would begin feeling fatigued and would succumb to a momentary illness. As strong as my body was, it would still take a week for me to fully recover.

After placing the ashes in the water, I opened up the pack and pulled forth the bougainvillea blossoms, all varying shades of purple. At first I gently sprinkled the blos-

soms over the ashes, some still floating on top, the rest submerged into a dissipating cloud. Then with my entire hand, J grabbed as many as J could, and threw them into the air, straight up. The air above me moved ever so slightly, gently dispersing the blossoms, spreading them out over the ashes. From family on the beach, the blossoms appeared to descend slowly like a magnificent gesture, making an everlasting impression to those who instinctively followed the blossoms to the ocean's surface. The event was dramatic to all who watched from shore.

Observing the ashes, J now wondered was this my brother floating before me or a symbol of him, or what? Certainly the ashes were his. This was his body in another state, but J began asking myself what was is it that makes us who we are. Certainly this was him before me, but not the same person J knew a month or so earlier. Through this process of transformation he had changed from how J previously knew him, but it was undoubtedly him before me. J soon expended my quickly diminishing energy and could no longer put forth any thought to the matter. Then J remembered the Ten Thousand Day learning process as Taoists view life and death.

Before J began the Ten Thousand days of learning, when J encountered death and dying, J did not weep. This is because J did not understand.

During the Ten Thousand days of learning, when J encountered death and dying, J wept. This is because J misunderstood.

After the Ten Thousand days of learning, I came to the Great understanding. And now when I encounter death and dying I do not weep. The reason for this is not because I say to myself that it is good not to weep, and therefore desist. I do not weep because death no longer disturbs me. This is because I have come to the correct understanding.

Treat life and death indifferently and all will then be clear. To treat life and death as separate entities is to set Heaven and earth apart. Tranquility comes from following what is natural. Life and death are cycles that are similar to the four seasons. We do not weep when someone dies for the same reason that we do not weep when the seasons change. To follow what is closest to nature is to follow the path to tranquility.

So many things, I thought, we accept at face value. We think we know what properties define a human being until we attempt to list these properties. Similarly a wave has many appearances, but defining its essential properties is something else altogether. It is not an easy task for even the best metaphysician, epistemologist or physicist.

Establishing the individual nature of ocean waves is not a simple task because of the intangibility of the entity we are dealing with. Quite simply, ocean waves are not usually thought of as things that can be touched, felt, and held, at

least not in the traditional sense of these terms. No doubt
that, for a surfer, a wave is something tangible, for it can be
touched and felt; but because the wave is motion within a
liquid, the task of holding it is more difficult.

When a set of ocean waves approach land, they will
eventually find their way onto a beach with a particular contoured bottom. Just as each of us has a unique and distin-
guishable form, the form of each individual wave is distinct
from the rest. This can be seen in the way the wave breaks.
But the material out of which the wave arises is the same for
all waves since each is rolling through the same body of
water, just as we are all made up of the same basic elements. Therefore, each wave's uniqueness rests on its form
rather than its matter. My brother's ashes were for all prac-
tical purposes formless. The ashes in the water were not his
Being. They represented his Being. This much was clear.
But I knew there must be something else to this inquiry.

When we say, look at "that wave," we mean, look at
"that particular wave." What enables us to distinguish each
particular wave is not only its form, but also the time between successive waves. This spatiotemporal separation
between waves is the wavelength, measured either from crest
to crest (the highest part of the wave), or trough to trough
(the lowest part of the wave). Without this separation between waves, no possible distinction could be made.

Accordingly what gives each wave its identity is wavelength (giving separation between waves), form (wave height
and shape), and matter (an ocean wave is a composite of
ocean water and small particles). But when we are com-
paring objects of the same substance, matter is irrelevant,

for all ocean waves contain similar particles. Similarly, we would not say wave #1 contains one type of particle and wave #2 contains another type.

When seeing my brother's ashes before me, I wanted to say that these were his and could not be mistaken for anyone else's. But the elements floating down before me would look the same no matter whose ashes they were. All human ashes are the same because our matter, our basic composition is the same. But as the waves flow over the reef, through the same body of water, I can distinguish one wave from the next without any difficulty. I can recall how one wave was superior in form to another over a long duration. I can recall the wave's clarity and color that distinguished it from the next, one time to another, before, during or after a storm. For only if there is a sudden change in conditions will waves that have been arriving at the beach murky-brown, eventually arrive crystal clear and blue. The coloring and the clarity do not depend on one factor alone. Each depends upon the type of bottom (coral reef, sand, cobblestone), the coloring of the contoured bottom, and water quality. These distinctions among waves are purely aesthetic.

Aesthetic qualities are determined by the original material. The materials mentioned above determine these aesthetic qualities of waves rather than the matter of the wave itself. The distinction that should be made then, is of primary/secondary qualities. This means that the "matter" that concerns us is not in the object itself (primary) but in the surrounding matter (secondary) that affect that particular object's identity e.g., the color of the coral bottom effecting the color of the water due to reflection.

We distinguish between waves by noticing their forms, the distance between waves, and their aesthetic qualities. A wave's form and aesthetic qualities depend on something external, i.e. the contour of the bottom. The color, clarity, and texture of the wave's surface depends on other things such as weather conditions and the color of the geological or marine material on the bottom. A wave is what it is, not simply because of the material that it contains, but also because of the interaction that takes place with its surrounding environment, the two never really being separated.

Distinguishing among waves requires examining both tangible and intangible entities and what each depends upon for its identity. Tangible entities depend on the primary characteristics, whereas intangible entities depend on secondary characteristics for their identity. This examines not just form but what the form is dependent on. It makes perfect sense to say that what the wave is, is a form rather than a parcel of matter. But this overlooks the aesthetic qualities. Once some of these qualities are removed, the entity would no longer be what it used to be; for an entity depends on certain qualities to make it what it is. If the coral reef were suddenly wiped out, the waves would cease to form as they once did. The wave interacts with the reef, enabling the wave to become the aesthetically pleasing form we see. One might argue that a wave's aesthetic value is contingent upon form and matter. But aesthetic value does not stem directly from form and matter in such a simple fashion. Aesthetics also depend on weather conditions that affect the surface texture of the ocean wave, and secondary external matter that the wave passes over.

Being able to distinguish one wave from the next is also dependent upon the empty space that surrounds it. The empty space between waves helps us to recognize that there are indeed individual waves coming in. Space that is empty is equally important, as a valley is the empty space between the mountains. To say that empty space creates existing entities would not be entirely correct, for the empty space does not directly create the entities themselves, but allows us the ability to distinguish them as being individual and particular. They coexist in a symbiotic fashion as Yin and Yang.

Matter alone does not always give an object its essence. In the waves, matter is constantly changing. In the ocean wave, flowing water is not constant to a particular location. Paraphrasing the familiar phrase from Heraclitus, "One cannot step into the same river twice." Obviously, the river is constantly flowing and no matter how quickly one reaches back in to touch the river again, one reaches back into different water. In this same fashion, I can not put my hand into the same wave twice while riding it, for the water is undergoing continuous movement. This simply displays the continuous change present in these conditions, and helps us to realize why matter in some cases can not be used as part of the criteria establishing an entity's identity. From examining waves with a new criteria in mind, I begin seeing them as more individual and distinct and understand the existence of the individual nature of waves.

This investigation has lead me to the nature of underlying essence. I could now see that the ashes in the water obviously could not stand as criteria for my brother's existence. This material before me certainly did not make him who he was.

To live is to interact, and part of my brother's existence was the pure interaction with the waves themselves. Riding waves with the natural rhythm of the ocean swells was essential towards defining who he was, as a wave becomes so, not simply being an ocean swell, but by the relationship it maintains with the reef it passes over as its raw and uninhibited energy pushes towards shore.

He was now a memory, but what else? That was the question to which I was now seeking an answer. What is our underlying essence? If the properties go unchanged throughout the transformations, then there is an eternal principle involved.

The ashes, the matter, were a part of him, but it certainly wasn't this that made him who he was, for even this material was in a constant state of change. Even when alive, he was constantly changing, from the internal changes that we notice in our health and fitness levels, to the external layers of dead skin cells that constantly renew themselves. He was the form, he was change itself. And now he exemplified the transformation of things. He was the Way I was searching for, guided by his state of Being, removing all separation, emulating pure and total immersion into the unknown levels of consciousness.

Chapter Four

Dancing upon the water,
Becomes the mystery itself,
Thereby unlocking all mystery.

– M. Anthony Allen

This is what it was all about: facing my fears, conquering them and going on now with the understanding J had always been seeking. After the weekend, the ceremony, and the scheduled events that followed, J now sit here, in my room alone, trying desperately to hear the waves just outside the window. For now, everything is very still, motionless. My usual sense of tranquility is far away, far but perhaps never totally out of reach. J finally allow the tears to flow.

J miss the waves we would ride together and that sense of camaraderie between the big wave men, a partnership and bonding given birth in the sea. Since the ceremony, the waves have been still, no movement at all. J don't think J've ever seen the sea so calm. This entire week the ocean has been flat, motionless. When someone passes away, we hold for them a moment of silence. When a surfer is buried at sea, the waves cease for the moment. Nature responds appropriately. The waves will arise once again when ready. Nature itself determines when that will be.

The nights have suddenly become cooler. Summer is coming to an end. I feel that even winter is not far off. The winds have changed, they're cooler now, more forceful, and they blow through the point uninhibited.

Crisp and fragrant mornings bring rays of light bending over the horizon, over the farms, over the mountains, now penetrating the bay. The beams disperse themselves through the few clouds that lie easily in the morning sky, floating, without movement. There is not even a breeze to disturb the call of morning. There is deep redness in the sky. "Red sky in the morning" is especially meaningful to the surfers who ride at dawn. The swell had picked up over night. It was the biggest swell yet of the summer, symbolically marking the ending of summer and the beginning of fall. The air is slightly cooler and soon the beach crowds will be gone along with the small summer swells. They will be gone too, and we can once again look to the western horizon for the coming of great things.

The wind dies as quickly as it came, as if it were being controlled by a switch on the wall. The sun enters through the clouds like royalty walking through a crowd of onlookers. The much needed warmth of the sun's rays returns to

me in an instant. I welcome every minute spent here on this
beach. The water is soothing to my feet. Still not fully re-
covered from the recent events, I go in no farther. I think it
best for the moment to stay dry and conserve the little warmth
I still have. The sand here is fine but hard packed, and it
squeaks as I move across it — an interesting sound that I
don't hear too often. My interaction with the elements on
this beach is psychologically beneficial.

Contrary to my original thought, I suddenly decide that
a quick swim would feel good before I head back. The light
breeze is still very warm, but in this late afternoon, the warmth
won't last much longer. I strip everything off and head out.
Turning around I notice a woman has followed my cue. She
joins me for a swim, a woman who I used to see now and
then, naked, on these beaches in the early fall of last year.
I thought she had disappeared, disappeared along with the
dream, the dream yearning for peacefulness, but appar-
ently not. We quickly get reacquainted. No clothes, no walls,
no barriers to obstruct, to interfere with my interaction. This
too is soothing to my mind and I feel more relaxed now. My
strength is finally returning. I am once again growing strong,
yet remaining very calm and at peace. This is the place to
which I will return.

The early morning mist falls heavy like small droplets
of rain. I sense the colder air throughout the night, indicating the arrival of fall, a season barely recognized by most
Californians. To surfers, however, this means a change in swell
direction, a change in winds, and a change in water temperature. It is time now for a warmer wetsuit. Even when my body
is at its strongest, I can endure only so much before I begin to

feel the chill right to the bone. With a high pressure inland, a low pressure off the coast, and swells coming in from the south, a day or two of unsettled weather may emerge.

Originating from a hurricane off the coast of Mexico, a new swell has reached the bay. The wind is offshore, the sun extremely bright, and the clouds an intense white, floating in an azure sky seen only when the wind blows out of the west. The air is tropically warm and humid. Images of a South Pacific island flash through my mind when I glance over at the few palm trees that grow along the point. When the wind blows out of the west, the air flow is picked up within the approaching waves. With each second that passes, the waves become steeper and hold until the top throws over all at once, creating a long, hollow cylinder.

From day to day now, I come to expect constant change in the weather. Only yesterday, the clouds that loomed overhead were ominous and dark and blocked out the sun until noon. When the sun finally broke through, its rays brilliantly illuminated each individual object against a black background of ominous clouds. Everything the sun touched stood out in dramatic clarity to the naked eye. Like exposed photographic film, my mind recorded and will long preserve those images.

Although my relationship is with the sea, even so I wanted to keep moving. I could never stay in one place for long, not happily anyway. I wondered if I could ever be anywhere for very long without feeling a desire to be back on the road. As good as the waves were out front, I would always want to continue my search and explore new breaks. But what of my relationship with others, could I ever find a partner for life. Could I stay in one place long enough? The most meaningful moments are oddly enough the most painful when I say I must leave, after caressing the inner beauty of our souls.

The waves now come in from two directions, the south and west, giving an occasional peak with outside sets lining up, usually too far to make. Consistency here now lies in the inconsistency of the form. The deeper meaning comes from the spontaneous movement in the beautiful unknown.

Labor Day has come and gone, and along with it, the tourists, crowded beaches, and noise. The air temperature has dropped some, and the water now seems warmer. The swell lines that hit the point are still obscure. The clean lines will gradually appear with the coming of winter. Why do I no longer mind the cold? It's as if I now welcome it. There was a time when the cold meant loneliness and the solitude of isolation. Although I do seek greater solitude now, I still feel I am a part of things, somehow tied in to something around me, the things that matter, the things that nurture my existence.

I can feel the coming of winter, I can smell the burning wood fire, and feel the cool evenings under the starry evening sky. At dusk, peacefulness descends upon the point and the beaches around the bay. The sound of the waves drifts without care to unexpected destinations. The salt air carries each note up from the beach to a little place hidden away in a dense grove, muffling extraneous noise. There, at this shack along the cliff, the moon penetrates the mist-covered foliage. The swell lines are visible through the trees as I pull a branch aside. Crisp eucalyptus leaves cover the ground like a tarp. I make my way across the railroad track. The train still runs through here. Mid- day I hear the gliding tonnage gracefully roll out each curve through the tree-lined cliffs.

Images flash through me of a time long ago when the wind swept beaches of my memory were warm and curiously waiting for interaction. The interaction I yearned for was with the sea and the friends I once surfed with, the old gang from a time remembered. I can't look back. Yet somehow I do without attaching myself to the past. A time came when I needed to break free. I knew others would stay behind. But I had to go. I took off so quickly, most never realized I had left until I was gone — long gone.

Mid-October. As quickly as hints of winter appear, it leaves abruptly, without a trace. A hot wind now blows down from the mountain. Indian summer has arrived. November is just around the corner and the wind blows like it did in the middle of July. As hot as it is, I am surprised that the swell is holding along the point.

Early mornings, however, bring a cool breeze. Before the sun is up, the air revitalizes my skin. I walk up along the point, feeling the air as it passes into me, into my skin, into my senses, into my memory. I prefer to protect myself as little as possible from the elements. I don't mind the cold, I

welcome it, J welcome what is natural in the changing elements of the seasons. J hide from nothing, J run from nothing. Why shield myself, why protect myself from reality? Too
much comfort and too much shielding from the external in-
hibits our ability to advance our knowledge and understanding of the worlds around us and within us. They maintain a
mutual and unavoidable interaction. Always keep warm,
always keep comfortable, never experience any discomfort.
Never experience the cold wind, winter's chill, and you live
apart from the world, separated and isolated from the real,
those things that let you know you're alive, that you can
feel, that you're unmistakably human.

The beginning of November. The wind that blows along
the bay is warm and calming. Nights are cooler and invite
warmer clothing. Days draw me to the sea. The solitude J
feel is warming to my senses.

J feel the ground shake beneath me with the surge of
pounding surf. The rest of the waves slip effortlessly into
the sand as if a million funnels waited onshore. The tide
rises, the ocean deepens and the waves slip deeper and
deeper under the surface, never to be seen again. The cliff
line continues to erode at an imperceptible rate. The cliff
speaks, warning of things to come. Jf we listen closely
enough, the voice becomes audible. The cliff is not alone in
its sensitivity. Anthropomorphize J must. Nature does speak,
if only we'd lend an appreciative ear. The slightest whisper
through the pines is significant. Listen carefully and we can

dispense with interpretation entirely, for what we will be hearing is the pure note, unaltered, uninhibited. The way of perfect communication — transcending all doubt we may have of reality, doubts that arose not from introspection, but from years of misunderstanding, miscommunication, because the ear was never lent. Had we only listened, had we been able to listen, we would have saved ourselves much trouble, much doubt.

The first storms arrive and do so in their usual way, without any warning. Mist settles in the higher levels of the forest overlooking the bay. It rains for moments off and on through the day, but when night falls, everything changes. The storm has turned into thunderous cloud bursts. I can't remember driving through a rain storm like this one. I slow down to a snail's pace and still can see nothing ahead but faint images. For a moment, things have become distorted as if driving through a dream, or perhaps just waking up from one. Dreams have always seemed clear to me, at least during the time that they were happening. But then, when I awoke, that was the time when I had to think about the dream itself, or soon lose it from my memory. Now, as I head down this highway, I flash back to times before, when I would recall something that fascinated me then, while not knowing precisely why. Peculiar as that may sound, I found that there was something that lured me into the unknown.

For a moment, the rain turns to hail. Ice pellets scatter across the hood and drop into the street. Patches of fog sit waiting without movement as the rain penetrates the ground-level clouds. As I continue over the mountain, people are pulling off to the side, but I know I must go on. I cannot stop now. I can neither cling to safety, nor to the possibility of what might happen. I have to go forth into the unknown. I must continue on.

Change in the weather has affected me. Waking to cooler air in the early morning brings back memories of a time long ago, a time when I was alone, cold and isolated, a time when I had to endure. It was a time of survival. But now, when I feel the cold, it summons not only memories, but an inner strength, it sparks an inner flame, and the warmth is brought forth from the core, the core of my thoughts as I rekindle the burning desire for continued development of the Self, development through experience, through understanding, through fine tuning my senses and my awareness.

I return to solitude. The cold is not harmful to me as it once was, as I once perceived it to be. The cool air that once brought me loneliness now brings me a sense of peace, a peacefulness that now runs through me.

I walk back above the beach, along the cliff, on the railroad tracks, alone, wandering without a care. My thoughts run free and flow smoothly down the tracks heading north. My thoughts focus on the here and now. They focus on the present, on the belief that if I maintain the present, the future will take care of itself.

Rain pierces the early morning sky. Now that it is mid-December, swells begin piling up on each other. As quickly as the swell ends, one is there to replace it. Whereas in summer, weeks could pass during which small waves became the norm, now rarely is there ever a single day of small waves prevailing.

The swells now are directed solely from the north. J remember back, back in time to a place that once was — a place of long ago. J used to be tied to the past, unable to set myself free, but J realize that my attachment wasn't to the people, it was to the land, more specifically, it was to the waves themselves. That's how J remembered a place, by the waves, by the contour of the land, by the images that would sweep through my mind like the tides that bring forth reflections in the sand. The waves were symbolic to me. And now, as J sit here, struggling to pull myself free, J wonder why the struggle exists at all. What am J pulling myself away from? J know that it was my usual way to head out on my own, leaving people behind, not expecting anyone to keep up with me, not expecting anyone to follow my path. Jf anything, J began to follow my self, my own instincts and intuitions. J guess all along J sought total non- attachment, wanting purely to trust my own thought. When the waves changed over time in the place of my youth, it was a reflection of the environment. This was plain to see, as plain as observing the movement in the wind.

Along the road, J head back from where J came, but never really returning to the same place. As each wave bends at a slightly different angle over the reef, J too view the world in a new light, extracting principles, grasping ideas, and redefining my existence. J gently glide over the reef, following the bending wave. The contours become my road as J continue to travel — without end — seemingly without end.

Without even thinking about it, like an intuitive glance, following instinctual patterns, J head out, back on the highway. Here, along the point, the wind blows onshore, creating a choppy ocean surface, slamming the waves into the cliff-line, but there, on the other side of the bay, things are different. As J drive pass the midway point around the bay, the air changes, the winds continue to blow as they did where J came from, but here, the wind is now offshore. One and the same wind blows, but this is the opposite side of the bay. The wind is now inviting, smoothing out the ocean surface, pulling the wave back as it begins cresting near the jagged shoreline. Here too, the waves break to the left as J look toward shore. How could J expect things to be the same simply because this is one and the same bay? Chaos and enchantment coexisting.

January has arrived, and for the moment, everything is still — the bay is quiet. The breeze that is usually present in the early evening has dissipated into air that moves about only as we move through it. The sun rests for a moment along the shore. The waves themselves are slow and graceful, moving with synchronized motion. The air cools as the sun once again sinks below the surface, leaving trails of light flickering through the darkened sky.

J wake the following morning to a sudden and distinct change in weather. The air moving about is restless, as if searching for a place to rest but not finding it. J glance through the trees and down to the beach and see the ocean surface rippled with swells moving underneath, rising as they approach shore, and then finally breaking, emitting and exposing their raw energy.

Although we are in the middle of winter, the sun's penetrating rays have perpetuated a sense of warmth throughout the bay. Other than the peacefulness of solitude on this beach, I feel that summer has never left me, that somehow I've captured its radiance and held it tight, pulled it into my soul, and tucked it away to be released at will. This radiance, this fire, burns brightly but effortlessly, emitting a glow seen when looking into the depths of my eyes, seeing beyond the surface, always looking beyond the immediately noticeable to capture the underlying essence.

When I first caught a glimpse, that's when the change occurred. It occurred both in me and in this object of beauty from which my eyes now stared, an image drifting across the infinitesimal grains of scattering sand. A startling reality faced me, and at the time I knew not what it was.

The radiance was in her, but it was locked up, buried deep, under layers of false promises. She had not opened herself up. The true self was stored somewhere within her, and at the time I doubt she knew of this herself. And so she continued to live a life as someone she was not. She became someone else, to survive. But surviving is what she was doing, surviving rather than living. The knowing and the understanding was not initially there, but came afterwards. But came in time it did.

Through the seemingly motionless waves of heat simmering across the sand, she continued on, finally disappearing into the great beyond, as if one could walk along these

beaches for eternity, as if she herself was eventually consumed by it all. Or perhaps she only existed in my mind for
the moment until finally deciding to leave and take up space
somewhere else, in what ever form she so desired. The heat
waves are haunting. They linger and give anything that
moves an eerie sense of distortion and disfigurement. I no
longer know what is real or tangible. I imagine reaching
out to something before me and having it slip through my
fingers, slip from my mind, and disappear without notice.
As I gaze toward the sea, the confirmation of what is real
strikes my momentary lapse of delirium and soothes my in-
stinctive passions for clarity.

January and February link together as clouds that drift
into one another leaving no evident lines of demarcation.
Rain continues to penetrate the darkened sky. But as the
clouds disperse, the sun appears while rain continues to
reach the approaching swells.

The wind blows through the open window as I drive
north. The wind continues through my hair, swirling through
the truck and quickly leaving me, back from whence it came.
Passing images no longer haunt me, but now live with me on
the road. Continuous change, I alternate my glances, to
the east, to the west, and continue on.
    March arrives, and with it a variety of seasons that
seem sifted together, everything at random, nothing in order
as we have come to expect it. That's precisely why I enjoy

it, why I never feel that I'm falling into a routine. The randomness and spontaneity send me along the path toward further discovery and understanding of the Self. I know that by adapting to randomness I've set myself apart from the rest, from those who allow themselves to fall into daily routines that slide into the meaninglessness of sameness. Repetition becomes mundane.

This is what I've been searching for, a deeper understanding of the Self. Without that, the journey continues into the unknown. The highway only becomes darker as one traverses through the hills that run along the coast, through the twisting lines that spill forth complexities in one's mind. I've driven this highway before and find that each time is like the first, where the understanding becomes markedly vivid, where deciphering takes place only when we can't free ourselves of the barriers preventing instantaneous perception through unclouded senses. So I make the journey again in an attempt to free myself of imposed barriers. No more baggage than necessary, minimalism, quality, the underlying essence. Excess gets in the way.

I wake up in a familiar place and soon head down the highway. The early morning has a certain feel to it. It's quiet and restful. The moon is nearly full and radiates its distinct image through layers of passing clouds. For the moment I never want to leave this highway. I continue down, catching only a couple of cars, neither of them close by, only the headlights beam down my path for a moment, and then disappear as quickly as they first came upon me. The air seems still and motionless even at sixty miles per hour. City lights flicker in the distance as an orange glow begins to emerge from behind the mountains that line the southern end of the valley. I'd rather get through or at least get into the valley before the sun rises, before the city awakens, the urban sprawl that winds around never really going anywhere. I'm locked in by a range of mountains, without which this place would not be what it is — a valley, separated from the ocean, from the bay.

Why there is fear in the unknown I don't yet fully understand. To live in the future, concerned about what has not yet happened, is a waste of precious energy. Living in the moment, I appreciate the here and now. I understand that the present disappears as quickly as I utter each syllable. Getting caught up in the future, of what could be, of what might be, or what may never be seems senseless. To appreciate the present moment allows one to understand the nature of things. Take care of the present and one takes care of the future. The future, then, never need be worried about. Alas, I take a deep breath and allow the air to fill me with wonder.

Now I stand here on our own land and gaze into the wispy clouds above as they pass so effortlessly. It is very peaceful here, and this is what I miss when I'm away. The valley is another place and time. I get caught up in doing so much there that I no longer have time to contemplate my existence. Except within me, I know that something isn't quite right, and I know that I must return to the shores along the Pacific. For it is there that my soul finds its resting place.

As summer approaches again, the waves no longer hold as much energy. The waves break with ease and roll forward in succession. The mornings are cool, the days warm and the nights bring a calming feeling to the air flow. I watch as the moon hovers over the point, and note the movement of the sea. I become fixed on the moon's reflection in the glassy pools.

In the early morning, the moon sits over the waves, providing ample light to surf by until hints of sunlight begin piercing the morning sky. With scattered clouds about, brilliant shades of orange and red drift across the sky. I gaze toward the sea. I realize this is a place that will always be with me, as the blood that runs through me. The swell lines pulse with each heart beat. A warm offshore wind winds its way along the jutting point. Before the sun finds its way over the mountain, I emerge from the waves and wander back home while the sun kisses the farms in the Salinas Valley.

If even for a moment my mind is troubled, now all thoughts wash away clean and give me a fresh perspective once again. Some things that were once of great importance now seem trivial. I focus on the essentials, realizing what really matters if I were to die in my sleep tonight. What is it that I will say, no attachment, no fear and no longer being of two minds: meaning no indecisiveness, no lies, especially to oneself, just a clean and concise understanding of the truth. This alone will set me free to roam on my continued journey.

Shifting, yet motionless, I dance across the reef, ever

so gently. The tide now is extremely low. Islands appear where I once rode days earlier when the tide was in.

My senses awaken in the cool water and again I ride alone. Being alone is how we find out who we are, our capabilities, our true understanding of the Self as we can know it now at our current stage of development. The coolness is invigorating to my soul, my senses are heightened, the sounds and smells add to the experience. I paddle in slow motion as if a strobe light were upon me. Each drop of water that I lift up with my hand as I raise it back out of the water, drops back from whence it came, each in succession. The first appearance of randomness is soon overshadowed by the existence of natural rhythm within spontaneous movement. Within spontaneity arises rhythm, beautiful sound emitted from each reaction to my own gestures.

The kelp beds themselves move in rhythm to the incoming swells. Flowing, with each successive movement from the winds, tide and rolling waves.

As with the sea in the aftermath of a storm, restlessness lingers with me. Searching elsewhere for the cause is fruitless. Restlessness with the wind is an indicator of an incoming swell and change in weather pattern. I wake to a slight breeze. The fog that was settling here along the point for the last few weeks has disappeared. I know that the valley is cooler since the fog wasn't pulled in along the coast during the night. The heat in the valley creates a vacuum effect, a low pressure zone that pulls in the cooler air from over the ocean. It condenses into a foggy mist as it meets with the warm air that lingers along the beach. Brilliant shades of grey and white clouds appear in patches, allowing intermittent rays to pierce through to the awaiting earth below. Seeing this is stimulating to my senses. For the last three weeks, the waves have been almost nonexistent as the fog remained motionless along the coast, only to finally burn off at some point in late afternoon.

I still find myself pondering the relationship I have with the sea. Therein lies a peacefulness that I can draw from, stillness, quietude. I have allowed myself to absorb what is useful to my Being. So too, I realize, when I become disturbed over things, I have allowed myself to become so.

Now it seems, I've come full circle, back to where I started. I know that in succession of a thousand times of returning, I'd return discovering that I had reached another level leading to a continually greater understanding. Returning to the same place where I surfed a thousand days, I'd never return as before. For in each successive time, I bring with me more experience and knowledge that was previously unavailable.

The cove where I placed my brother's ashes into the calm waters of the bay only a year ago is where I find myself once again or perhaps I've been continually discovering myself and the cove has merely become a symbol, a symbol that can be reflected upon at will. For it is no accident that I have returned here.

The wind is cool and passes through me as if I were the variable that it was seeking to go beyond, way beyond, and then to look back from which it came, utilizing me as a marker of sorts. As if I stood for something. As a lighthouse guides ships around the point, I provide the guidance to myself as I continue on this journey. Never a fol-

lower. J choose my own course of action, and then take full responsibility for it. J choose my course and live with it. J live well within my means, finding the middle ground between excess and defect, neither too much nor too little, not an exact point but a range that takes into account existing circumstances. For not all similar situations arise in like fashion.

How is it that J have come to where J am now, living simply, trying to always maintain simplicity in living, and doing so within a complex system. Perhaps J have made the system complex, or further yet, perhaps there is no system except that which we ascribe to it, impose on it. We, as a race of humans, continue looking for systems, as if these systems were out there waiting for our grasp. Jf we only knew where to look, or if we looked hard enough, we'd find them. What then? No doubt with systems prevalent, we conclude order, or at least some type of order which satisfies us. No matter a system's inherent complexities, we can derive further knowledge from a system that we've come to understand based on our own imposed beliefs and subjective interpretations.

Underdeterminism, a philosophical system not unlike the Tao, flows with our continuous growth of knowledge. The "system" is merely a tool used to go from one point to the next, never rigid, pliable, and flowing so effortlessly, totally unlike any fixed system. Jt is the element of the unknown, so it seems, that does so throw a hint of obscurity into the furnace. A fixed system can always define, never leaving the possibility for an unknown, whereas the flexible system's goal is not to define all, but rather to shed light onto the subject at hand, to bring forth greater clarity without falling into dogmatic rhetoric.

When presented with an unknown, we react by defining it, thinking that this process will lead to a better understanding. If an unknown remains, it remains as something that we can never rest peacefully with. Taoism seeks a greater understanding but does not seek to define. Any definition, no matter how elaborate, will have limitations, and of course, being too elaborate, and too encompassing will entail the loss of validity. To define a flowing movement is like trying to harness movement itself. And what is "natural rhythm" but a sequence of events which seem to us, linked in some way? Yet the links allow for this movement, a movement that generates a spontaneous flow at which point we call it "natural rhythm". If we were to understand death in the light of naturalness, then perhaps there would be less fear. For even though there may still exist unknowns, we can feel more at ease knowing that death and naturalness are equated. After all, what do we mean by naturalness, but events that occur as they would without our intervention?

The air is warm and still, the sand hot to the touch, beads of sweat drip from my brow into the sand, each drop evaporating upon contact. The waves too, have become motionless and nonexistent. Stillness is reflected everywhere. The water here maintains only a degree of clarity. These are dirt cliffs with soft limestone that pulls apart at the simplest grasp from my fingers. It's lightweight and so mixes with the current and flowing movement of the tides, never resting.

The other side of the bay is granite. It too breaks apart, but the weight of each grain is much heavier; a coarser and denser grain. Even with the wind, tides and moving currents, the grains sink to the bottom, or find a place to rest on the shore, leaving the water aquamarine. Very few particles are light enough to remain in an aimless, wandering state. The search continues for increased clarity.

Clouds scatter as the day comes to a rest. Moonlight seeks to penetrate each layer of obstruction. Nothing will interfere with the moonlight and the waves becoming one, finding inseparability throughout the night.

The time for change becomes remarkably clear. Not only my body, but my mind prepares for the coldest part of winter. My mind-set is different. My thoughts reach to the past and pull from it ideas and events. I reexamine things I never fully understood in hopes of gaining greater insight.

Still the wind is warm in late afternoon, but the temperature of the water fluctuates from day to day.

As the dead of winter nears, the weather becomes much colder, but now I no longer feel so cold. I recognize that in the past, during previous winters, I nearly froze. But then, my mind wasn't as it is now. There was too much conflict before, thoughts taking control of my will, rather than willing my own thoughts. But there was much to sort through and my troubled state set me toward one path, to become of one mind, no longer being troubled by doubt.

Now, I walk outside into the cold night with a warm feeling. I feel a sense of belonging. I feel in touch with the environment and no longer feel the separation that once existed within me.

The cold. Isolation itself is cold, loneliness is cold. Now I'm by myself, but I no longer feel alone.

I suppose feelings of isolation have dissipated because of my relationship with the Self, and my relationship with the sea. Each is harmonious, each lends an ear, each listens attentively and each responds in its own way, a unique way, echoing the pattern of simplicity.

Simplicity is a patternless pattern, formless in its individuality. Each breaking wave is a form comprised of ten thousand forms and so can never be duplicated, not even by the wave following immediately after. Individuality begins like the wave, a formless form. Simplicity arises out of complexity.

Trees continue to fall from the saturated soil and high winds. The roots no longer have a hold and so lean with the wind, eventually uprooting themselves. Runoff into the rivers is tremendous, as the ground can absorb no more. The once trickling streams are now potent rivers that run their course to sea. The river-mouth continues to widen at the entrance to the beach. The beaches themselves are barely recognizable, appearing nothing like they did even a month before. Where I once strolled easily in summer is now pounding surf, gradually climbing its way up the beach. With each successive high- tide, the ocean pulls farther and farther in, redistributing the sand, reshaping the beach, reforming the

land. The waves shape not only the land, but continuing to
reshape my existing thoughts, forming new ideas, redirect-
ing my path.

Each time I ride, each time I pass through another
wave, I seem to hear his voice. It follows, watching over
me, bringing me to safety. My brother's voice is clear. How
could I not sense his presence. He is there with me before
the sun rises as I paddle into the waves. The waves are
black silhouettes which become noticeable by the reflection
of the moonlight. The swells roll toward home. I sense a set
rolling through, turn around and go, paddling to the sound
of the breaking wave. Suddenly I drop, not knowing how
steep it will be at first, but glide down with my instincts guid-
ing me. Looking toward the shoulder, the reflection of light
flickers in the face of the wave, dropping and rising as the
wave changes shape over the reef. Now I ride with the
moonlight as my guide, sensing the speed, sensing the form,
a formless form that is ever changing. My board travels with
precision as I make my way down the line, carving, pulling
into turns as I drop farther down the face, turning and once
again pulling into the wave as it now steepens over a shallower part of the reef. My alerted instincts are heightened.
The ride seems endless as I continue on, constantly moving
and flowing, finding the natural rhythm that each wave seems
to possess. The wave begins to close out as it suddenly hits
a section of reef only a few inches deep. Quickly I turn up
and pull out through the lip as it passes over me, nice and

easy. Now I can see. Even within darkness there is light. The blackness of night has now become visible.

This morning, the water feels cooler, more invigorating and stimulating to my senses and yet it was calming. Cooler water and air are calming because I associate them with the seasons, the seasons which are quieter, less populated and slower paced. Usually summer is associated with a time to relax, but I see overcrowding, and too much going on. People try to get here and there, as if they are on a schedule that needs to be strictly followed. I thought, how can I relax, how can anyone relax while being on such a strenuous schedule? Often they try to do far more than is possible in the time allotted. When the schedule appears, the spontaneity disappears, and with it, freedom and flexibility. So much is at our grasp if we only allow it to appear before us. We end up roadblocking the things that could bring us to the places where we want to be. The irony of it all. Some of the very things that we look so hard for are often waiting there for us, waiting for us to grasp and pull toward us. But in doing so, there should be no struggle. For it would seem odd if it were a struggle to obtain greater peacefulness. Or would it? Perhaps like seeking a structured system, the struggle is self-induced, self-imposed onto something that might otherwise contain a flowing movement. Some may say that "great things don't come easy." But peacefulness like other things that we call great become so when compared to things that we consider to be of lesser value, and so the comparison arises. However, what if peace of mind were never given a value. What if it is what it is, peace of mind. If we never allowed our minds to come to the point of unrest, then peacefulness would be a constant Way. Then things would be in order as Taoists maintain.

Despite the coolness of the early morning fog, I stroll into the water and plunge myself under a wave lunging toward shore. The cool water is invigorating. It provides a clearer picture as it brings me closer to reality. Warm water has always been pleasant. But being pleasant does not draw me toward higher levels of awareness. I seek the knowing aspect. "Knowing" itself is active and ever-changing as it moves with the real, the ever-changing reality of the external world, what we properly term phenomena. But warm water does not move me into the real. Pleasantness brings forth a dreamy state of relaxed solitude. But a continuous state of anything without change leads to a lack of pliability and adaptability. It seems to also prevent any further developmental awareness of the world, and more importantly, of the Self. Lying on the beach can be both relaxing and stimulating to my mind where I can ponder new ideas that spring forth. Even with this pleasant atmosphere, I can only stay on the beach so long before I must again return to the water. Invigorated, I land in a foamy bath of white water, remnants of the wave's arrival to shore. Water is soft and pliable, but carries energy that can erode the hardest of stone. Each time I emerge from the waves, I feel that somehow a bit of this energy remains with me. In the emerging itself, therein lies a transformation. So often, I emerge alert as a warrior. My senses are heightened. I feel calm and at peace. Not only do I experience a physiological transformation, but my level of consciousness is altered as well. It is as if now I can take on whatever comes my way, as if no task could ever be too great. The thoughts that I ponder before entering the water are cleansed and wiped clean, as if while surfing I have reached into a wave and pulled forth the answers to my questions.

The final answer that came was that not all questions need be answered, some not answered immediately, some need never be answered at all. I can rest well with that, for not in every case does a question necessarily require an answer. At times, questions are posed only to bring forth more reflection. It is obvious that some questions bring forth only more questions and this not need bring dismay either. These questions should instill greater insight, leaving us with more understanding about ourselves, rather than leaving us in the dark, thinking that we have merely walked away with an unanswered question.

In the evening, I'd stand at the edge of the cliff, look out upon the water and watch the swells. I'd feel the direction of the wind as it reached into me, and passed through me as if I wasn't there. At times, I stood motionless against the silhouette of the moon as it danced over the waves. Early on, my relationship formed with the sea. I continue to remind myself of this, wondering where it began, wondering about the origins of my relationship. In attempting to fulfill this search, my mind wanders back to the moments that still remain fresh, moments that are symbolic of my journey. For only in searching back to my origins with the sea will I uncover the reason for my continued exploration.

   The realization became suddenly, manifestly apparent. My brother was returning to the "natural state." In the beginning, this expression seemed so clear to me, so close to me. But the more I thought about it, the more I became unfamiliar with it. Like many things that we become familiar with, we may have a tendency to overlook the underlying truth. This truth only lay hidden because we haven't taken the time to observe, to listen, and to understand. In this case, I realized that the term natural state was something other than I had first envisioned. I was thinking of it as being an expression of calmness, something I would equate with tranquility. On this point, I was headed on the right track. But I went astray when I associated it purely in psychological terms. The tranquility was not simply a state of mind. Rather it was a state of Being that transcends life and death, timeless and eternal. Then I realized that his ashes now floating in the bay was not only the most peaceful of scenarios but was the root of our origin, our very beginning, where our relationship with nature is complete and inseparable. He was closer to nature than I would ever be by riding the waves alone. How much more joy could there be than to return to this natural state of Being. As the wave is not a wave on its own but becomes so with the interaction of the reef, so too will he enter this pure relationship never separated from nature. Interaction brought forth his essential Being. Interaction was the key that released the once mysteriousness of Tao.

Tao is pure interaction, not harmony of opposing forces but rather interactive qualities that support each other and nurture each other in a symbiotic sense. The ocean swells and the coral reef possess qualities. When the swells pass over the reef, these qualities become "interactive" in a sense that there is an exchange of attributes. Each quality is being redefined. During this interactive process, each quality is no longer what it was. With the exchange of attributes, the original qualities become more than they once were. It is not that the reef itself becomes greater because it is surfed over, but the interaction gives rise to new qualities that could unquestionably not exist without it. The phenomena lies in the relationship where the interaction is taking place. The wave takes on its particular form due to the reef that it passes over. And the reef is no longer simply living organisms sprouting new life and existence, but also becomes the "shaper of ocean swells." These forces shape each other, for with each passing wave there are turbulent forces absorbed by the reef.

As my brother rode the ocean swells, he and the waves shaped each other. They interacted and developed a relationship that gave rise to greater existence. The inner qualities each possessed were transformed. This phenomenon was inescapable. For no longer are the observer and the observed separated as was once thought. The significance of the transformation was not purely aesthetic, an altering of external qualities. It also shaped our perception of our-

selves and of our environment, and as a final result, our
perception of the world. The transformation of qualities in-
dicates that we transform each other. Powerful forces blend
into harmonious interplay, a unifying process which gives
birth to redefining our existence. The process is interaction
itself, an ongoing process, and is perhaps one without end.

If our bodies experience 10,000 transformations as we
walk over the land, as we gaze toward the sea, why then do
we shed tears when death itself is only another phase of
transformation? Not for the person, if we come to understand the meaning behind the Taoist interpretation of death,
but from the grief we feel from our own loss, not being with
that person any longer. Yet this thought did not seem altogether correct either.

I remember telling my brother that we'd surf together
again and felt that his presence would never leave me, that,
in a sense, he would be watching over me while I surfed. I
thought that some day when I was near death myself, when
I was pulled under the waves, he would suddenly pull me
up and out of the water, back up to the surface once again,
acting as a guardian angel in some respects; or would be
there for me when I decide this will be my last wave, feeling
it's time to go. I had hoped to see him again while surfing,
and still hope that I will. Maybe if I am expecting an image
of him to appear I will be sadly disappointed. If a feeling of
his presence is with me, then perhaps he has never left, and I
need search no more.

Indeed, he has returned to that from which he came, to
the pure interaction, the origin of our Being — to the waves
themselves.

Afterword

Upon completion of this book, I shared a copy with Dr. Paul Tang, who served as the chairman of my Master's thesis committee. He brought to my attention that there were some areas that might need elucidating, thereby providing the reader with a greater understanding of particular concepts as well as to obviate superficial views on Taoism that arise from its popularization. It became clear to me that I needed to review such terms as Tao, Wu-wei, Being, Self, and natural state, examining each of these in its historic place of origin rather than from its insignificant and most often incorrect meaning drawn from a popularized status.

Back in 1990, the book was still titled simply "Tao of Surfing." One day while pondering the title and what the book was meant to accomplish, I came up with the subtitle, "Finding depth at Low Tide," which parallels Taoist writing utilizing linguistic paradoxes. I met with Dr. Richard Bosley, a prominent Canadian philosopher in the patio of a small cafe in Santa Barbara, California. With our shared excitement about the subtitle, the book was able to take on new meaning allowing for the synthesis of ideas that led to its eventual completion.

The book was originally written, however, not with the intention to publish, but simply because it was something I had to write for myself. I still hold fast to the belief that a true writer who writes from the heart writes solely for that reason, therefore making the task of writing a good in itself. But with my promise to my brother that I would dedicate the book to him, coupled with the overwhelming enthusiasm I received from persons reading the manuscript from all walks of life, I was eventually convinced that this reflective and introspective "Journey" was one that needed to reach a wider public. I soon realized that this journey would become a personal one to each who had the courage to venture into the pages and allow themselves to literally be swept into the natural landscape.

To elucidate upon some key words, one will notice that I use Being with a capital "B" as part from "being" with a lower case "b". Being with the capital "B" signifies one's essence. In the literal sense, it is what you are as an individual, that which separates you from all other individuals. Hegel, a 19th century German philosopher illustrates this point to a tee. Being with a capital "B" is the pure essence, that which defines our individual existence. Being, is in a sense, always in the process of becoming because it is continuously redefined as we continue to learn and grow. This process I call self-cultivation. The term "self-cultivation" is self-descriptive. It merely refers to one's continued progression. To use the phrase, "cultivation of the Self", however, leads to another sort of philosophical investigation entertaining a new set of ontological questions. What is the "Self" and how do we know when the "Self" has been cultivated? To adequately answer this could bring forth another book in itself. For our purposes, however, I think it suffices to say that the "Self" is used in the same sense as when we say, "myself," as in myself displaying possessiveness of identity, ownership of individuation. It is your Self and no one else's.

Determining to cultivate oneself should not be an arduous task. Self cultivation has its origins in Chinese philosophy over two thousand years ago with both Confucius and Lau Tzu. The former focusing on oneself within the social environment and the latter focusing on oneself within the natural environment. Both, however, give rise to heightened understandings of our place in the world.

Tao, pronounced "Dao," is a term originating in the Chinese language. The word itself, however, is undefinable. To attach a name to it, to attach a label to it is to notice the name and not the entity. As the famous Zen saying goes, "One may point his finger toward the moon, but once the moon is recognized, the finger is no longer needed." It is as Being was to Hegel, true undefinable existence which ultimately must remain nameless if it is to retain its own pure essence. But for purposes of communication, we ultimately do name it.

Regarding translation, philosophers will tell you that some of the essential meaning will always be lost. Tao is often translated as Way with a capital "W". To risk coming across dogmatic and self-righteous, Tao displays the Way as elucidating "the Way of nature." No matter which way that is, it is distinctly the way of nature itself. In an attempt to understand and establish that there indeed exists order in the universe, scientists have developed theories and principles which eventually lead to what they term as, "laws."

Laws translate into Taoist terms as "ways of nature."

Another term associated with Tao is Wu-wei, incorrectly translated as "non-action." "Effortless action" would be more appropriate, otherwise Taoism becomes misinterpreted as a philosophy of passivity which is hardly the case. Taoism is more a philosophy of action and movement but it is the type of movement that distinguishes it from other philosophies of action. Taoism emphasizes simplicity and the flowing movement within the natural course of things. In other words, as the stream flows down from the freshly melted snow, a boulder that stands in its path will not stop the stream from flowing. The stream will naturally redirect its course around the object that was once in its path.

Emphasizing simplicity, it avoids complication. Simplicity itself in its pure form is the natural state. To return to the "natural state" is to return to the uncarved block, the uninhibited Self that is free from worry and fear, walking through life without rigidity, with minimal needs and concerns. Hence my discourse on nakedness as a metaphor symbolizing the stripping away of external baggage that eliminates our ability to truly "interact" with our environment.

Taoism also utilizes seemingly paradoxical sayings as in, "within motion, therein lies stillness, and within stillness, therein lies motion". These messages are not self-contradictory but provide a level of higher consciousness in thought. Naturalistic metaphors are also very much a part of Taoism. These rich metaphors serve not only to heighten our sense of awareness but also serve as tools useful in developing a new way of viewing ourselves and the world around us, our Weltanschauung. "Death as natural as the four seasons," for instance, is psychologically soothing and actually gives rise to a new perspective. As I have tried to illustrate in my writing, Taoism brings forth personal identification without losing its underlying essence.

In ancient Chinese texts, the usage of "Ten Thousand," as in Ten Thousand Days, means a long period of time. It is used as meaning a great many when no specific number is attached. Clearly, these ancient texts carry with them rich, naturalistic metaphors providing a poetic tone to the reader's ear with the inherent quality of transcending all barriers.

About the Author

Michael A. Allen

Photo by Julie Allen

Michael Allen holds both a Bachelor's degree and a Master's degree in philosophy as well as a certificate in Asian Studies from the California State University at Long Beach. While serving as President of the Student Philosophy Association, he chaired the session, "Medical Ethics," for a seminar on Applied Ethics. He has presented numerous papers on Chinese Philosophy. In 1989 he lectured on Taoism at the International Society for Chinese Philosophy at the University of Hawaii.

His interest in Chinese Philosophy led him to travel extensively through the People's Republic of China while attending the International Society for the Philosophy of Science. Upon his return from China, he published his Master's thesis on East-West comparative philosophy. He then packed his truck and headed for the central coast of California, where he was able to teach philosophy and begin intense work on Tao of Surfing. Still feeling the need to be back "on the road," Michael decided it was time to see America. Spontaneity winning over his rigorous schedule, he took Amtrak around the country, finally returning to finish writing the book.

He continues his studies in the Chinese language and is avidly working on a novel. Michael Allen has been surfing for over 20 years. Recently married, he and his wife live along the central coast of California.

Tao of Surfing:
Finding Depth at Low Tide

by Michael A. Allen

Additional copies of "Tao of Surfing" can be had by

–   calling, toll free, 1-800-356-9315, Visa/MasterCard/
    American Express/Discover accepted.

–   faxing, toll free, 1-800-242-0036, Visa/MasterCard/
    American Express/Discover accepted.

–   sending $12.95, plus $3.00 shipping and handling, and
    applicable sales tax, to Rainbow Books, Inc., P. O. Box
    430, Highland City, FL 33846-0430.

–   asking your bookseller for ISBN 1-56825-057-6

Information on bulk purchases can be had by contacting

Rainbow Books, Inc.
P. O. Box 430
Highland City, FL 33846-0430
Telephone/Fax (941) 648-4420
Email: Naip@aol.com